BIG BOOK OF

SOLITAIRE

BIG BOOK OF
SOLITAIRE

Francesca Parodi

Sterling Publishing Co., Inc.
New York

Library of Congress Cataloging-in-Publication Data Available

Edited by Rodman Pilgrim Neumann
Quadrille, Spider, and *Yukon* by Sheila Anne Barry

2 4 6 8 10 9 7 5 3

Published 2004 by Sterling Publishing Co., Inc.
387 Park Avenue South, New York, NY 10016
Originally published by *Artemesia Progetti Editoriali*
under the title *Il Grande Libro Dei Solitari*
English translation © 2004 by Sterling Publishing Co., Inc.
Distributed in Canada by Sterling Publishing
℅ Canadian Manda Group, 165 Dufferin Street,
Toronto, Ontario, Canada M6K 3H6
Distributed in Great Britain by Chrysalis Books Group PLC
The Chrysalis Building, Bramley Road, London W10 6SP, England
Distributed in Australia by Capricorn Link (Australia) Pty. Ltd.
P.O. Box 704, Windsor, NSW 2756, Australia

Sterling ISBN 1-4027-0944-7

For information about custom editions, special sales, premium and
corporate purchases, please contact Sterling Special Sales
Department at 800-805-5489 or specialsales@sterlingpub.com.

Contents

INTRODUCTION

ORIGINS OF CARD GAMES
AND OF SOLITAIRE

The true origins of playing cards are obscure and, perhaps, that has encouraged many countries to take credit for inventing them. The most widely accepted theory places their origin somewhere in Asia. A Chinese dictionary, the *Cheng-tzâ-t´ung,* first published in 1678, states that in 1120 during the reign of Hsüan-ho in the Sung dynasty, an imperial decision was requested to establish which of several forms of the game now known as *T'ien-kiu* ("Heavens and Nines") was to be considered orthodox. This is understood to indicate that the game, and the cards, must have been in existence long before.

The date of the appearance of cards in Europe is a matter of dispute. Boccaccio (1313–1375), Chaucer (1343–1400), and Petrarch (1302–1374), who often talk about games in general, never mention card games, which seems to indicate that in their times card games were almost unknown.

Giovanni Covelluzzo of Viterbo, in the fifteenth century, claims that cards were brought to Italy from Arabia: "In 1379 the Moors imported to Viterbo a card game called Naib. It is known that the crusaders, passionate players, have imported card games. According to other opinions, however, card games first appeared in Spain, having been imported by the Moors."

A first sure mention of playing cards can be found in the notes of Charbot Popart, treasurer of Charles VI of France, in his household expense accounts from 1392. His notes refer to payment to Jacquemin Gringonneur for painting three sets of cards—which were evidently already well known.

At the end of the 14th century the use of cards had become common, up to the point that, in 1397, the provost of Paris issued an edict prohibiting the people from playing card games, among others, on working days. It is certain that card games were familiar to Italians, since in 1423 Saint Bernardine of Sienna (1380–1444) held a famous sermon in Bologna against their use.

There has been a lot of discussion about the place where the first deck of cards was produced. Nevertheless, the coincidences between the first European packs and the Chinese cards are thought to be too numerous to be accidental.

The earliest European cards were hand painted, but wood-engraved cards appeared in Italy in 1425, and cards from Germany from the 1440s were already printed using wood blocks. Hand-painted cards appeared in England in 1463.

Europeans experimented with the structure of playing cards, particularly in the 1400s. In Italy it appears likely that the Tarot deck, originally (and still) used for the game of *Tarocchi,* was invented at that time. Court cards were changed to represent European royalty and attendants, originally "king", "knight", and "knave" (or "servant"). Queens were introduced in a number of different ways. Throughout the 1400s, 56-card decks were common containing a King, Queen, Knight, and Valet.

There were usually four suits: in Germany these were called Hearts, Bells, Leaves, and Acorns, while in Italy and Spain they were known as Swords, Batons, Cups, and Coins. The present-day variety of Hearts, Diamonds, Clubs, and Spades originated in France, in approximately 1480, and was widely adopted in the 16th century. Playing cards are thus commonly referred to as French cards, although they were imported to France originally from Italy.

It is more difficult to establish the origins of solitaire games. History does not shed any light on their origin, but we can state, without fear of being wrong, that solitaires were likely born at the same time as decks of cards. But the passion for this type of pastime is much more recent than the invention of cards, and reached the epitome of its development in the time of Napoleon Bonaparte. He was a great aficionado of solitaires, and many games bear his name, although it is unlikely that he invented them, since in some cases a game with his name did not even exist until after his death.

Solitaire, defined by France's Noah Webster, Emile Littre (1801–1881), as a game that develops into "diverse combinations of cards which can be executed by only one person," is also called patience. The outcome for some games depends on luck, but others involve real skill and judgment. Solitaire is in any case the perfect game, one in which you are competing only against yourself and the run of the cards.

SOLITAIRE TERMS

Available
Available cards are the cards that can, in accordance with the rules, be moved from one pile to another, onto the tableau, foundations, or spaces.

Blocked
When you cannot find any more moves to make, you are blocked or stuck.

Build
To build is to place one card on another to create a sequence, according to what the rules of the specific game call for. See pages 12 and 13 for details.

Cards
The solitaires presented in this volume are played with a simple deck of 52 cards (jokers are excluded). In the few cases where a game requires the use of two decks, or where certain cards are removed from the deck (then called a "stripped deck") before play, the description of the game explains this. Before starting the game remember to properly shuffle the cards.

By convention, cards are made 3½ inches high in two widths: 2½ or 2¼ inches. There are also novelty cards of various sizes and shapes, including round cards. We advise Solitaire players to buy special narrower cards, because they occupy less space on the table.

Colors
By color we mean red or black. Hearts and Diamonds are colored red, of course, and Spades and Clubs are colored black.

Foundations
Foundation cards are the first cards of certain piles onto which, according to the rules of the specific game, sequences of cards are built. They are usually cards of a specific rank, often Aces, that are typically put above the layout, but are sometimes placed differently. Usually the foundations are empty at the start of a game, but in some games they are part of the layout. The goal of most solitaire games is to move all the cards onto the foundations.

Layout
The solitaire game starts with the distribution of cards on the table in a prescribed pattern, or tableau, that varies from game to game. This pattern

together with any other cards dealt out at the beginning of play form what is called the layout. The layout is the set of cards at the very start of the game, when you are ready to play but have not made any moves yet. For the elements of layout, see page 11 for details.

Pile
A pile of cards can be squared, spread out in a fan, or empty as a space.

Rank
The rank is the number value of a card. Usually the Ace counts as one and is the lowest-ranked card. The rank of the cards increases from the Ace up to the King. The Jack, Queen, and King count as eleven, twelve, and thirteen, respectively.

Spaces
These are gaps, or vacancies, in the layout into which cards may be legitimately played, or, depending on the rules for the specific game, they are places where cards have been removed and they may or may not be reoccupied.

Stock or Remaining Deck
This consists of the cards that remain in your hand after the layout has been dealt. Various rules establish whether you need to draw them one at a time or according to a certain order (for example, three at a time).

Suite
A full set of thirteen cards of one suit, from Ace to King.

Suits
A 52 card deck has 13 cards of each suit: Hearts, Spades, Diamonds, and Clubs.

Tableau
The tableau is essentially the layout once the game has commenced. The tableau piles are your workspace, being the cards you move back and forth while you look for opportunities to transfer cards to the foundations. Generally the game is built on top of the tableau.

Wastepile or Reserve Deck
This consists of cards that do not find their places on the foundations or on top of other cards in the tableau. They are often dealt faceup in a pile on the side. Only the top card of the wastepile can be moved onto other piles, thus entering the game, according to the rules of the specific game. This "reserve" of cards is not part of the tableau, and so cannot be built onto.

MAIN ELEMENTS OF LAYOUT

Row
A series of cards placed horizontally, parallel to the edge of the table in front of the player, is a row. The row is always formed starting from the left to the right. If a second row is called for in the layout, the cards should either overlap the first row or be placed clear horizontally below, according to the layout for the specific solitaire game.

Column
A series of cards placed vertically on the table in front of the player is a column. The column is formed starting away from the player, and comes toward the player ("down") card by card. If the cards are arranged in more than one column, the cards should be placed clear or overlap, again according to the layout for the specific solitaire game.

Squared Pile
This is a group of cards (the number of which is indicated precisely by the rules of the game), that is, placed on the table as a set; the upper card completely covers the one underneath. In some cases a pile of cards is dealt so that it is not squared but spread out in a fan; most typically they are spread down.

Fan
A pile that has been spread out so that all of its cards are visible, is called a fan. Only the topmost card of the fan will be completely visible, the other cards being overlapped. Fans may be spread right, left, up, or down.

Deal
Distributing the cards is dealing. You deal the cards to create the original layout or to add cards to the tableau.

BUILDING SEQUENCES IN SOLITAIRE

The purpose of solitaire is to build sequences by placing the cards on top of each other, either on the foundations or in the tableau. There are various ways to build.

You can build without taking the suits into account
In this case you don't take into account the suits of the cards underneath (for example, an eight of Hearts can be placed on top of a nine of Clubs).

You can build while taking the suits into account
This means that a card of Diamonds, for example, can be placed only on top of another card of Diamonds in a sequence, according to rules the specific game.

You can build according to color
Red cards can be placed only on top of red ones; black only on black ones.

You can build using alternating colors
Only a red card can be placed on top of a black one, and the other way around. In many solitaires alternating red and black is the most frequent case.

You can build up
This is the normal sequence—it starts with the Ace and ends with the King:
a) According to suit: this means, for example, that a 10 of Hearts can only be placed on top of a 9 of Hearts.
b) According to colors: this means that a red 10 can only be placed on top of a red 9, for example, or a black 6 on a black 5.
c) Without taking into account suits or colors: this means, for example, that any 10 can be placed, independent of suit and color, on top of any 9.

You can build down
This is a sequence that starts with the King and ends with the Ace:
a) According to suit: this means, for example, that a 6 of Hearts can only be placed on top of a 7 of Hearts.
b) According to colors: this means, for example, that a red 6 can only be placed on top of a red 7, and the same goes for black cards.
c) Without taking into account suits or colors: this means, for example, that any 6 can be placed on top of any 7.

You can build up and down in different columns

Depending on the rules of the specific game, you might be able build some columns in ascending order and others in descending order. Such rules are indicated separately for each game.

You can build up or down at given intervals

The most common example is building in twos: that means placing the 3 on top of the Ace, and then the 5; or the 4 on top of the 2, and then the 6; thus building columns of either odd or even numbers. These rules also are indicated separately for the specific game.

The way to build is evident for each solitaire according to its specific rules. Typically, one or more cards, which are placed in different piles, allow another card to be placed on top. The card being placed on top of another card in the tableau may be alone or it may be the top card of an entire column. To move an entire column, it is the card at the top, therefore, that must belong on top of the card in the tableau. For example, if in the game we have, starting from the player, a sequence of 6, 7, 8, 9, 10, this sequence can be taken as a block and placed on top of the Jack, which becomes the head of the column. In another game the rules may only allow the last card in a sequence to be moved; for example, for the sequence mentioned above (6, 7, 8, 9, 10) only the 6, the card closest to the player, can be moved and placed on a 7 in the tableau.

SOLITAIRE

GAMES

AGNES

☞ *(Triangle)*

ORIGIN: American
DECK: 1 deck of 52 cards
TIME: 10 minutes
DEGREE OF DIFFICULTY: ☆ ☆ ☆

Layout

Form seven rows of cards faceup, starting close to you and moving up: in the first row place only one card, in the second place two, in the third place three, and so on until you reach the seventh row consisting of seven cards; this way you will have built a sort of triangle. The 29th card of the deck will be the foundation, and is placed at the top of the tableau.

How to Play

The last card of each column, closest to the player, is the only one that can be used, and can be placed either on top of the foundation or to form descending sequences, building down on top of another final card, without taking into account the suit, but only black on top of black and red on top of red.

As you are able to form sequences, these can be moved toward the interior. As soon as an empty space appears, try to place a King in it, preferably choosing the free space, on top of which you will be able to place the largest number of cards in sequence. To continue play, you deal another seven cards, one at the lower end of each column. All seven must be dealt onto the table before you can move any of them. You are allowed to deal seven cards three times, then you will have two cards in your hand. Turn them faceup; they are then available to play, too.

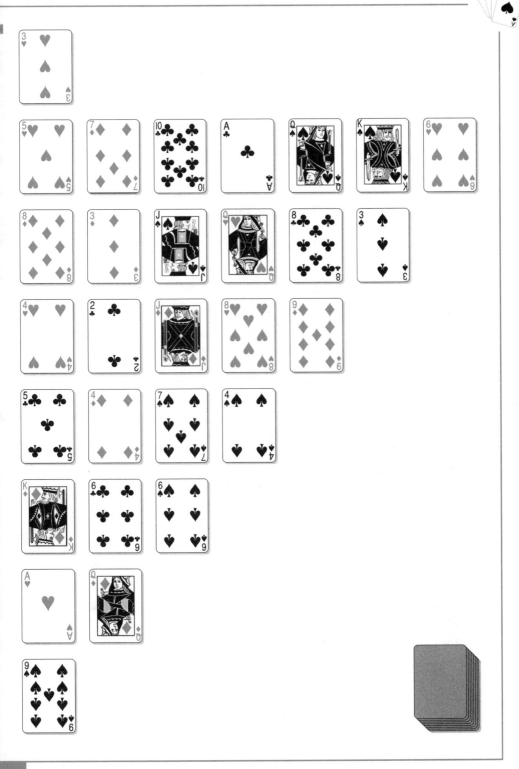

ALHAMBRA

ORIGIN: Italian
DECK: 2 decks of 52 cards
TIME: 10 minutes
DEGREE OF DIFFICULTY: ☆ ☆ ☆

Layout

Select from the deck an Ace and a King for each suit and place them in a row at the top; these cards are the foundations. Underneath the row of foundations, deal eight piles of four cards each. Only the top card of each pile is playable.

How to Play

Build up on top of the Aces and build down, in descending sequences, on top of the Kings, always following suit. The cards of the remaining deck are placed facedown on the table and then are drawn one by one. If they are not playable, they are placed in a wastepile to the right. The wastepile can also be built on top of either up or down, according to suit. Each card played on the wastepile can be ascending or descending, as needed. For example, an Ace can be placed on top of a King or be under a two. The top card of the wastepile is always playable. You are allowed to redeal the wastepile twice.

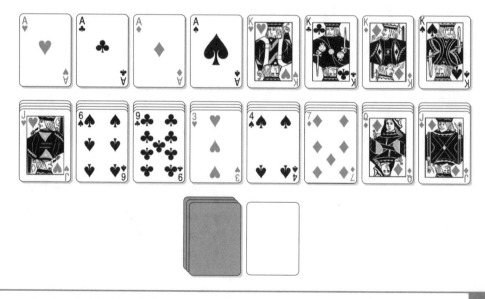

ARMORY

☞ *(Arsenal, Deposit)*

ORIGIN: French
DECK: 1 deck of 52 cards
TIME: 5 minutes
DEGREE OF DIFFICULTY: ☆

Layout

Select the twos from the deck and arrange them in a row at the top of the tableau; these cards are the foundations. Then create an "armory" or "deposit," actually a pile of thirteen facedown cards that you place to the left, and deal four cards faceup in a row below the foundations.

How to Play

The foundations are built up, in ascending sequences, according to suit; the Ace will be placed last, in this game it is the card of the highest rank. To play, turn faceup, one by one, the cards of the armory and, if possible, move them to the foundations or play them in descending sequences, always according to suit, on top of the cards of the tableau. When the card is not playable, place it faceup in a wastepile. If a space is freed on the tableau, fill it with a card from the deposit, the topmost card of the wastepile, or another card from the tableau, but you cannot move the cards that are on the foundations. When the armory is exhausted, deal another pile of thirteen cards from the stock. When they are both exhausted, play from the wastepile, turning the cards over one by one. The wastepile can be turned around twice.

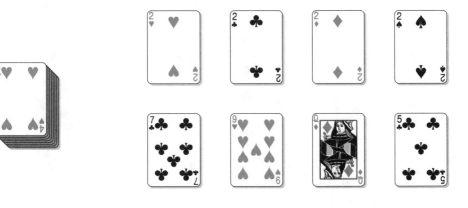

AULD LANG SYNE

ORIGIN: British
DECK: 1 deck of 52 cards
TIME: 2 minutes
DEGREE OF DIFFICULTY: ☆ ☆ ☆

Layout

Select the four Aces from the deck and arrange them in a row faceup; these are the foundations onto which you can build up to the King, without taking into account the suit. Below the row of Aces, deal another row of four cards.

How to Play

When you have finished the moves you can make with the lower row of four cards, deal another row of four cards right on top of them. Keep going until the stock is exhausted. The only way you can play cards that have been covered in the lower row is by playing the cards on top of them.

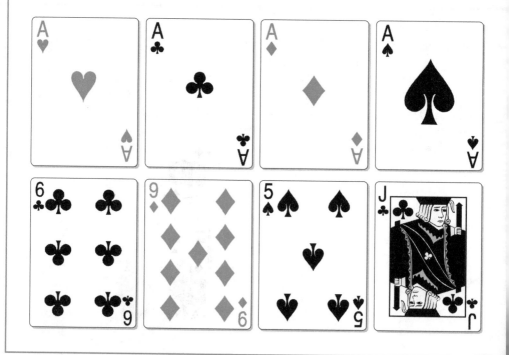

BAKER'S DOZEN

ORIGIN: British
DECK: 1 deck of 52 cards
TIME: 15 minutes
DEGREE OF DIFFICULTY: ☆

Layout

Deal 13 columns of four faceup, overlapping cards. After you lay out the cards, check on the Kings. If a King is in an exposed position, move it underneath the other cards in the column. If a King is lying on another card of the same suit, place it underneath that card.

How to Play

When the Aces become available, arrange them in a row at the top of the tableau; these are the foundations upon which you will build up to the King, following suit. On the tableau, however, you will build down, regardless of suits and colors. You can only lift one card at a time and place it on top of another pile. You can fill spaces with any card, as long as it is on top of a pile, or you can choose not to allow spaces to be filled.

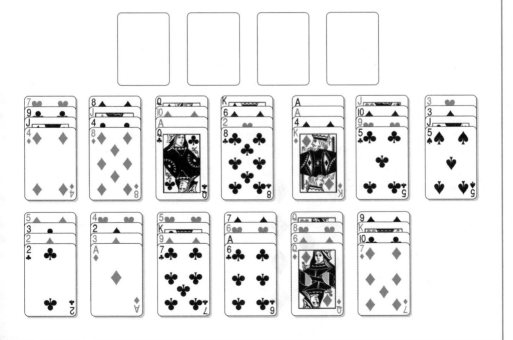

BARONESS OLGA

☞ *(Catherine the Great, Seven for Seven)*

ORIGIN: Russia
DECK: 4 decks of 52 cards
TIME: 30 minutes
DEGREE OF DIFFICULTY: ☆

Layout

From each deck remove the twos, threes, fours, fives, and sixes of each suit. Lay out the cards, dealing seven rows of seven cards each (in total 49 cards) with alternating rows faceup and facedown (see the layout opposite). These are dealt left to right in rows from top to bottom.

When the Aces show up (sixteen in total), arrange them in two columns, to either side of the tableau. These are the foundations. Aces that show up while you are laying out the tableau must be placed immediately in the foundations, but you cannot build on them yet. Any empty space thus created in the tableau while it is being laid out must be filled with other cards from the stock before continuing the layout.

How to Play

Build up following suit on the Aces. Note that the Ace is the lowest card and the next card that needs to cover it is the seven. All cards that are faceup are playable; you can build down in alternating colors onto the faceup cards in the tableau. You can move single cards or ordered piles on top of other piles. Note that each column alternates from a faceup card to a facedown card; as you play, when a card that is facedown becomes the bottom card of a column because a card faceup underneath has been removed, the facedown card can be turned and is then playable. As spaces develop, however, you can move Kings there that might otherwise prevent a facedown card in the row above it from being turned.

When no more moves are possible, draw from the stock, one by one. If the card is playable, place it on a foundation or in the tableau; however, if it is not, form a wastepile, of which only the topmost card is usable.

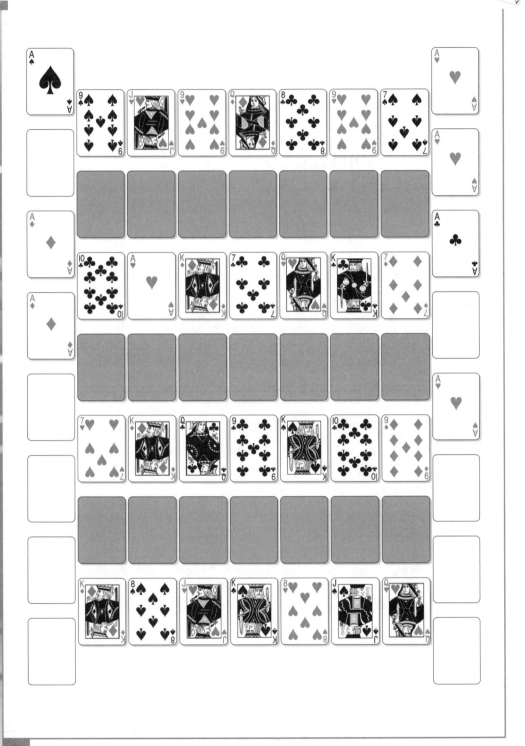

BELL

ORIGIN: Italian
DECK: 1 deck of 52 cards
TIME: 20 minutes
DEGREE OF DIFFICULTY: ☆

Layout

Select from the deck the four Kings to be the foundations, and deal the remaining cards faceup in six rows of eight cards each. Place the Kings at the top, two at the left and two at the right.

How to Play

Like the swinging of a church bell which sounds now from one side and then from the other, the columns of this solitaire are playable first from the left (ding) and then from the right (dong). The cards are playable to the opposite Kings or the bottom of the tableau. On top of the Kings you form sequences in the following order: King, Ace, two, etc., up to the Queen. In the tableau, sequences can be built down, following suit, only on the cards at the bottom of a column—that is, the bottom row or one in a row above that is freed by moving the card immediately underneath. You can also move an entire sequence to the card immediately above in the same column. For example, if in the development of the game you have placed on top of the seven of Hearts the six and the five of the same suit, you can then place the little pile on top of an eight of Hearts that is directly above.

Once you have distributed the layout, you can play the cards from the left to the bottom cards of the tableau or the right Kings, thus making the first sound of the bell, "ding." When all moves are made, you can then play cards from the right to the bottom cards of the tableau or the left Kings, "dong." The bell keeps "ringing" as long as there are moves to make. When no more moves can be made, the game is blocked; you are allowed to pick up the tableau cards, shuffle, and deal again, but only once.

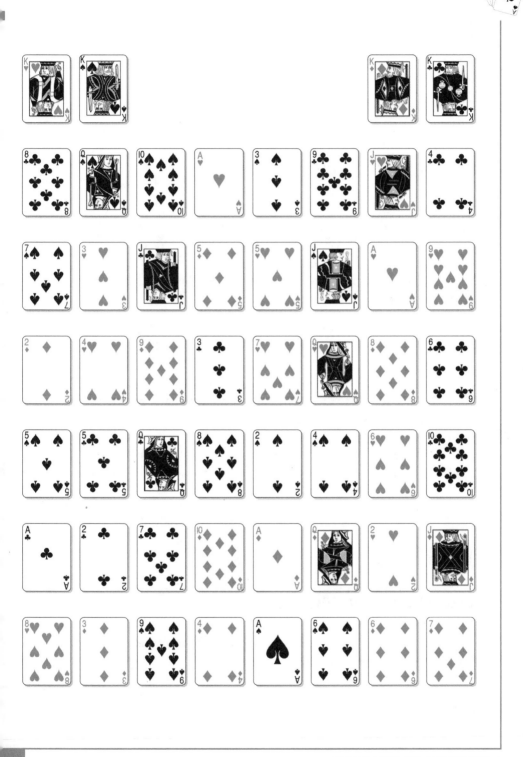

BESIEGED CASTLE

☞ *(Beleaguered Castle, Fortress, Day of Maneuvers, Sham Battle)*

ORIGIN: French
DECK: 1 deck of 52 cards
TIME: 15 minutes
DEGREE OF DIFFICULTY: ☆

Layout

Select the four Aces, which are the foundations, and arrange them in a column at the middle of the tableau. Deal out the rest of the cards faceup to form four wings at the left and the right of six overlapping cards each. Traditionally this is done by dealing the cards in columns of four, alternating left to right.

How to Play

On top of the foundations, build up to the King, following suit. Only the fully exposed cards are playable, and only one card can be moved at a time. On the tableau you can build descending sequences, regardless of suit. When a wing is freed, you can move one card into that space. For the success of this solitaire it is important to carefully analyze the moves before making them, pondering whether by moving a card you ruin the possibility of making moves on the tableau and easily building sequences. The goal is to place all the cards on the foundations.

BESIEGED CASTLE 2

DEGREE OF DIFFICULTY: ☆ ☆

In order to make this Solitaire more difficult, and thus more captivating, build the sequences on the tableau in either ascending or descending order, taking suit into account. The foundations are still only built up following suit. Cards on the foundations are, as always, never playable; however, you can move the ones on the tableau any number of times.

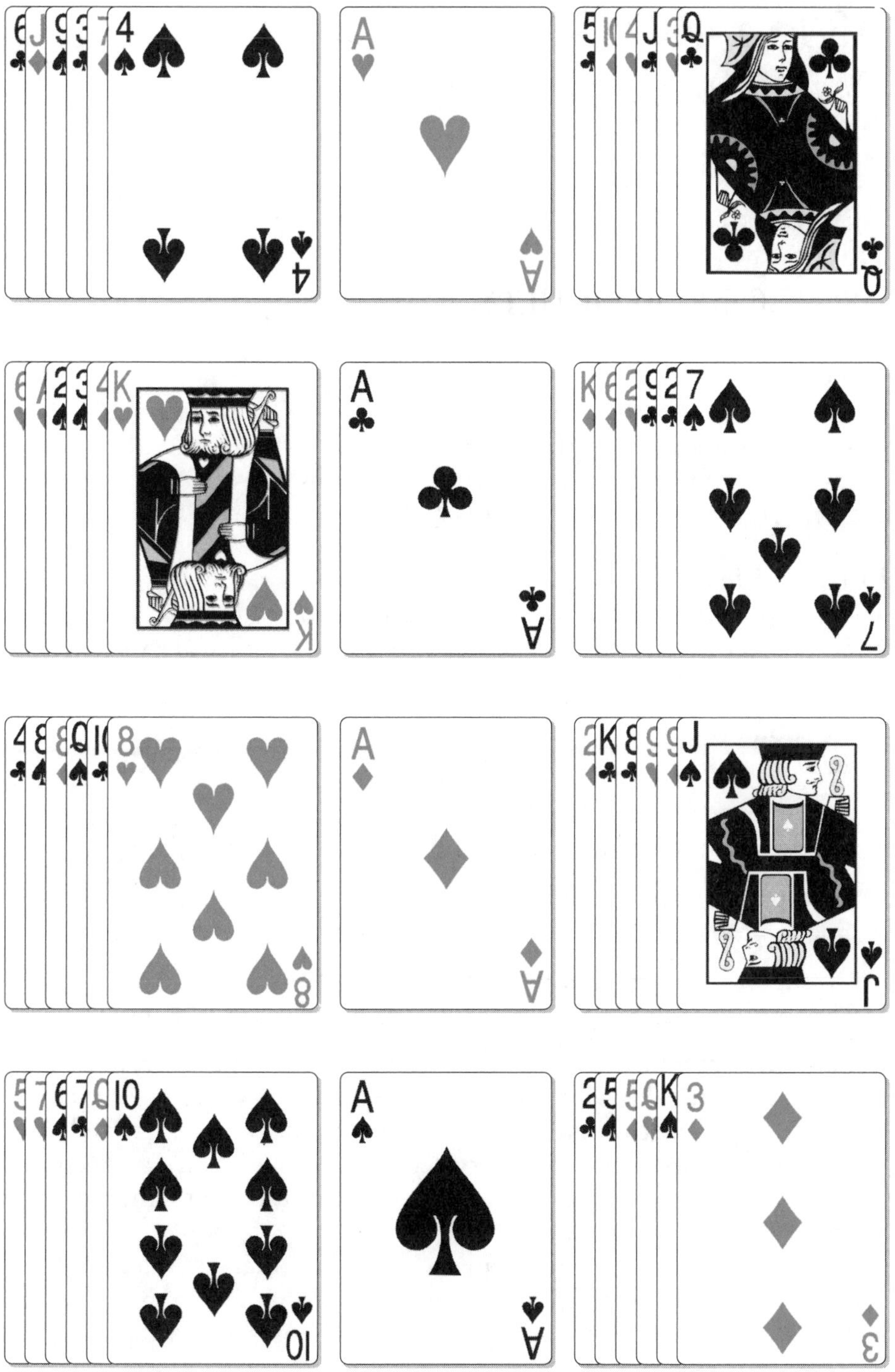

BETSY ROSS

☞ *(Musical, Fairest, Plus Belle, Four Kings)*

ORIGIN: American
DECK: 1 deck of 52 cards
TIME: 5 minutes
DEGREE OF DIFFICULTY: ☆ ☆ ☆

Layout

Lay out a row of cards consisting of any Ace, two, three and four. In a second row directly beneath, lay any two, four, six and eight. The bottom four cards are the foundations. You'll be building on each of them up to the King, but in an unusual sort of way.

How to Play

The only function of the top row of cards is to remind you of the key numbers you have to build by. You will build up, regardless of suit, in the following pattern:

On top of the two, you build in the standard way, by ones:
three, four, five, six, seven, eight, nine, ten, Jack, Queen, King;

On top of the four, you build by twos:
six, eight, ten, Queen, Ace, three, five, seven, nine, Jack, King;

On top of the six, you build by threes:
nine, Queen, two, five, eight, Jack, Ace, four, seven, ten, King;

On top of the eight, you build by fours:
Queen, three, seven, Jack, two, six, ten, Ace, five, nine, King.

Cards are drawn from the stock one by one and, if possible, placed on the foundations, otherwise they will be placed in a wastepile, of which only the topmost card is usable. When the stock is exhausted, the wastepile becomes the stock for two more turnings. You can keep the cards of the wastepile spread out so you can see each of them, but only the topmost card is playable.

A variation allows four wastepiles, one below each foundation. This allows you the added strategy of deciding into which waste pile to place a usable card from the stock. The ordering of the wastepiles then becomes crucial to your success.

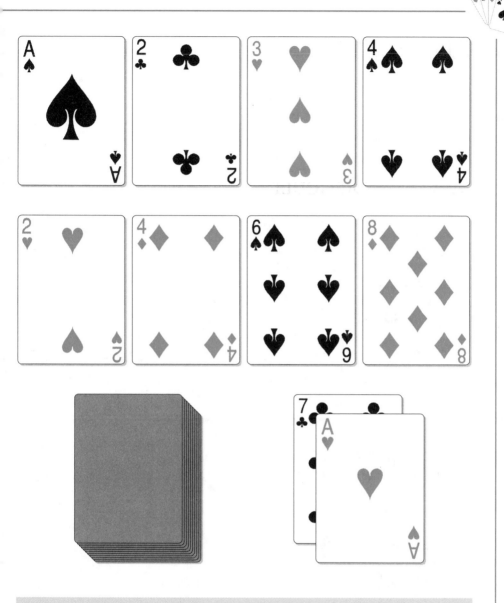

Did you know?

This solitaire takes its name from the embroiderer who sewed the Stars and Stripes, the flag adopted as the first national flag of the United States of America. This game dates in fact from the time of the Declaration of Independence in 1776, and is also called Fourth of July in celebration of the birth of the new nation.

BIG BEN

ORIGIN: British
DECK: 2 decks of 52 cards
TIME: 20 minutes
DEGREE OF DIFFICULTY: ☆ ☆

Layout

This game has a beautiful layout, its only drawback ibeing it requires a lot of table space. The space is necessary in order to see the possible moves as soon as possible. Select cards from the deck to arrange at the hour numbers of a clock dial (as you see in the drawing below) in the following manner:

Six of Clubs for 1;
Seven of Hearts for 2;
Eight of Spades for 3;
Nine of Diamonds for 4;
Ten of Clubs for 5;
Jack of Hearts for 6;
Queen of Spades for 7;
King of Diamonds for 8;
Two of Clubs for 9;
Three of Hearts for 10;
Four of Spades for 11;
Five of Diamonds for 12.

Around the clock, deal 12 piles faceup of three cards each, one pile for each hour.

How to Play

The twelve cards of the central ring are the foundations, the piles at the exterior are the tableau. You construct ascending sequences on top of the foundations, following suit, until the rank of the top card indicates the hour (for example the two at the nine o'clock position needs to be covered up to the nine). The totally visible cards of the tableau are playable and can be moved on top of other piles, always one at a time, or by building upon the hours, whichever you prefer. These cards, however, should be in ascending order, following suit: the King is followed by the Ace and then by the two. Each group of cards in the tableau should be formed by at least three cards; when you move a card from any pile, you must restore the pile to three cards by dealing one from the stock. When no further play is possible, you can turn the cards of the stock, one by one; those that are not playable are discarded in a wastepile, of which the topmost card always stays playable. When the stock is exhausted, deal cards from the wastepile to restore a minimum of three cards per pile.

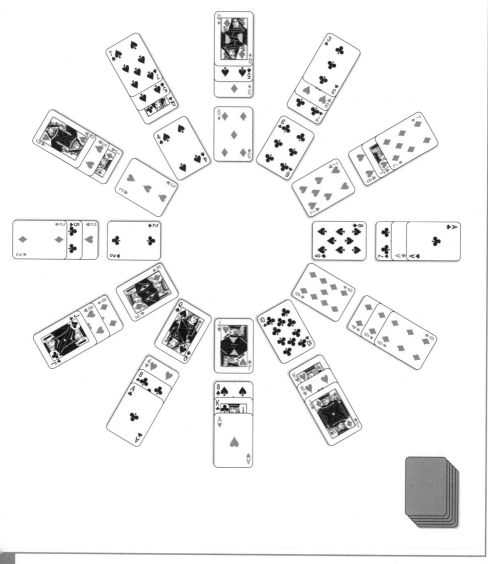

BLACK PANTHER

☞ *(Belgian Congo, Moojub)*

ORIGIN: Belgian
DECK: 1 deck of 52 cards
TIME: 5 minutes
DEGREE OF DIFFICULTY: ☆ ☆

Layout

At the left of the tableau, deal a column of four cards, which are the reserve; the card of the lowest rank is positioned in a second column, at the right of the one of the reserve and will be used to form the column of foundations. Replace the missing card of the reserve from the stock. Underneath the first foundation place a second card, which needs to be the lowest card you in the reserve but of a different suit than the first one. According to this principle, display the third and fourth cards in such a way as to form a column of foundations with the cards of different suits and of the lowest rank possible (the very lowest card is the Ace, whose rank is one).

How to Play

Build up on the foundations, following suit; when a sequence arrives at the King, you can continue with the Ace of its suit and then proceed with the two, three, etc. If possible, form a second and a third column of foundations: the number of the foundation columns is up to you, and the cards can be placed there as they show up in the reserve. The free spaces of the reserve are always filled with cards from the stock. When the game is blocked, deal four other cards on top of the four cards of the foundation; only the topmost card of each pile is playable. The game is successful when all cards have been placed on the foundations.

BLOCK

ORIGIN: British
DECK: 2 decks of 52 cards
TIME: 15 minutes
DEGREE OF DIFFICULTY: ☆

Layout

Deal two rows of six cards to form the tableau. When an Ace turns up, place it in a row at the top of the game; the Aces are the foundations upon which to build sequences.

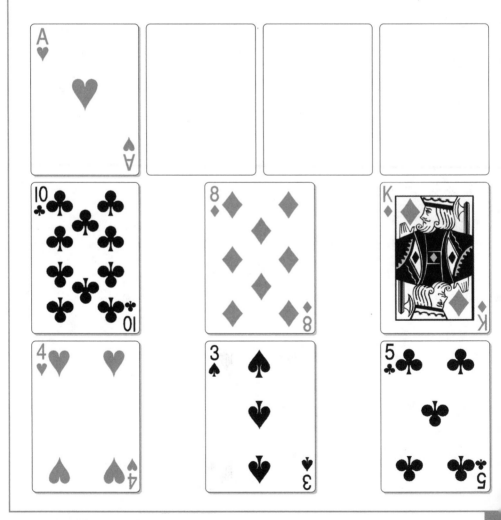

How to Play

On the Aces build up to the King, following suit. Play all possible cards from the tableau to the foundations, then fill the empty spaces with cards from the stock. When there are no other possibilities, deal two rows of six faceup cards directly on top of the first two rows; only the topmost card, however, may be played. Now you can build down, always following suit, on cards of the tableau, filling any spaces with cards from the stock. The game is completed successfully when all cards have been moved to the foundations.

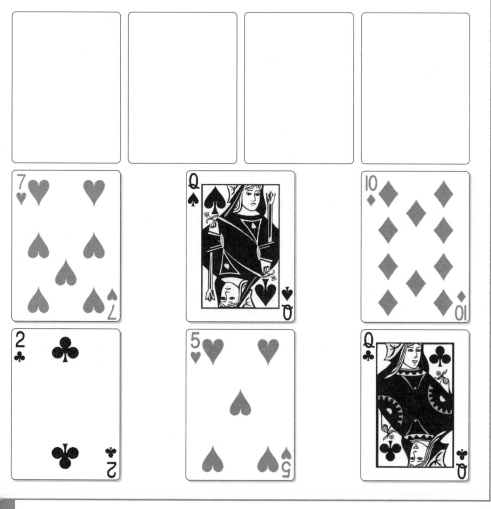

BOOMERANG

☞ *(Indian Arch)*

ORIGIN: American
DECK: 2 decks of 52 cards
TIME: 5 minutes
DEGREE OF DIFFICULTY: ☆

Layout

Remove the threes, fours, fives, and sixes from the decks. Then arrange twelve cards to form the tableau, placing them in three rows of four cards each. When you encounter the sevens, place them in a row at the top of the tableau. The sevens are the foundations.

How to Play

You build on the foundations according to suit in the following order: seven, eight, nine, ten, Jack, Queen, King, Ace, King, Queen, Jack, ten, nine, eight, seven, Ace. Each card of the tableau can be moved, individually, on top of another card or pile, in order to build a sequence either in ascending or in descending order but always following suit; however, the order of construction for each individual pile can never be changed.

Keeping in mind the sequence of the foundations explained above, in the tableau an Ace can be placed only on top of a King and a seven can only be placed on an Ace. The free cards of the tableau can be played to the foundations. Fill empty spaces only with cards from the stock. The cards from the stock are drawn one by one.

For a successful game it is a good idea to look carefully at the next card of the stock before playing it in the tableau, on the foundations, or in an eventual empty space. When no further moves are possible, the game is finished. It is better to build on the tableau in descending order, if possible, because if you use those cards to build in ascending order, you will later find it almost impossible to place all the cards.

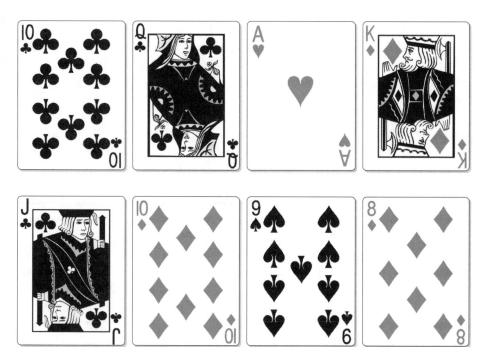

BRAID

☞ *(Plait)*

ORIGIN: Italian
DECK: 2 decks of 52 cards
TIME: 15-20 minutes
DEGREE OF DIFFICULTY: ☆ ☆

Layout

Lay out nineteen cards in the shape of a braid at the center of the tableau. To each side of the braid deal six cards, four of which are vertical and two of which—the top and bottom—are horizontal. Having finished the layout, turn the first card of the stock and place it at the bottom of the braid; it becomes the foundation.

How to Play

On top of the foundation, build ascending sequences (Ace following King and preceding two), regardless of suit. The playable cards are the cards of the two side columns, the cards of the stock, or the last card of the braid. The cards of the braid can be moved only to build the sequence on the foundation, or when a free space is created in one of the four corners. If a free space is created where there had been one of the vertical cards in the two columns, it is filled only with a card from the stock.

When two cards are playable on the foundation at the same time, and one is in the braid and one in a column, the one of the braid is always given priority. The stock is turned one card at a time. Unplayable cards from the stock are placed in a wastepile, of which the topmost card is always playable. You can deal three times, after which you are still allowed five cards. If after these you have not managed to place all suits on their foundations, the game is blocked.

A variation has the first card of the stock becoming one of eight foundations. The first foundation card then determines the rank of the other seven foundations. The sequences on each foundation must then follow suit and end with the card that is below the first foundation card.

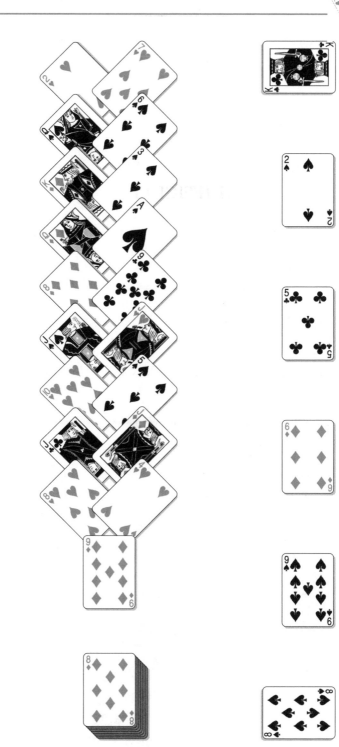

BRISTOL

ORIGIN: British
DECK: 1 deck of 52 cards
TIME: 20 minutes
DEGREE OF DIFFICULTY: ☆ ☆

Layout

Deal eight fans of three cards each faceup in the tableau. As you deal, any Kings that turn up in a fan are moved to the bottom of that fan pile. Below the fans deal a row of three more cards faceup to form the start of three wastepiles or reserves. As soon as the Aces show up, they are set out in a row above the fans as the foundations.

How to Play

On the foundations you build up to the King, without paying attention to suit or color. On top of the fans you build down, also without taking suit or color into account. Only one card may be moved at a time; you cannot move the sequences from one pile to the other. The stock is dealt three cards at a time—one card to each of the three wastepiles. Spaces are not filled again, except from the stock to the wastepiles. You are only allowed one deal.

BRUSSELS

☞ *(Round, Perpetual Clock)*

ORIGIN: Belgian
DECK: 1 deck of 52 cards
TIME: 20 minutes
DEGREE OF DIFFICULTY: ☆ ☆ ☆

Layout
Deal thirteen piles of four cards each faceup on the tableau; each pile is assigned a number in order, from one for the first to thirteen for the last.

How to Play
The goal of the game is to succeed in moving the topmost card of the first pile onto the second one, the topmost card of the second pile onto the third one, and so on. A pile becomes blocked if the topmost card has the value of the pile (see below: the three of Clubs is on the third pile); in this case you skip that pile and place the card in the next pile. When there are thirteen cards matching the number of their corresponding piles, you remove those cards and restart the game. Continue removing cards until you obtain three sets of thirteen cards, and a set of thirteen cards remains on the tableau.

CALCULATION

ORIGIN: Russian
DECK: 1 deck of 52 cards
TIME: 15 minutes
DEGREE OF DIFFICULTY: ☆ ☆

Layout
Select from the deck an Ace, two, three, and four, without regard to suit and arrange them in a row. These are the foundations.

How to Play
Build ascending sequences on the foundations, regardless of suit, and according to the following pattern:

On top of the Ace:
two, three, four, five, six, seven, eight, nine, ten, Jack, Queen, King;

On top of the two:
four, six, eight, ten, Queen, Ace, three, five, seven, nine, Jack, King;

On top of the three:
six, nine, Queen, two, five, eight, Jack, Ace, four, seven, ten, King;

On top of the four:
eight, Queen, three, seven, Jack, two, six, ten, Ace, five, nine, King.

The stock is drawn one by one and placed on the foundations or below in one of four wastepiles, of which the top card is always playable.

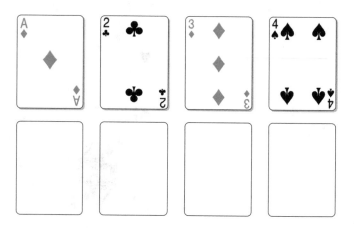

CANFIELD

☞ *(Demon, Thirteen, Fascination)*

ORIGIN: American
DECK: 1 deck of 52 cards
TIME: 10 minutes
DEGREE OF DIFFICULTY: ☆ ☆ ☆

Layout

Deal out a reserve pile of thirteen cards (twelve facedown and the thirteenth faceup). Then place the fourteenth card above to the right of the reserve, as the first foundation; it sets the rank of the foundation cards for this deal, and as soon as the other cards of the same rank appear place them in the foundation row. Finally deal a row of four cards to the right of the reserve.

How to Play

Build up on the foundations, following suit, until you form piles of thirteen cards each; the Ace goes on top of the King and below the two. In the tableau row, however, you build down in alternating colors. The topmost cards can be moved to the foundations but not to a free space, while whole sequences can be moved to another pile. Any space that is freed is filled from the the reserve. When the reserve is exhausted, you can refill it from the stock or the wastepile. The cards in the stock are dealt in batches of threes, keeping them in order. The topmost card of each group is playable, as well as the ones underneath that become free in the process. The cards that are not playable are placed in a wastepile, the topmost card of which is always available for play. You can redeal the wastepile up as many times as you want, or until the game is blocked.

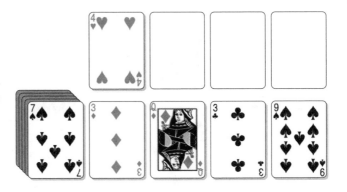

CAPRICIEUSE

☞ *(Italian Caprice)*

ORIGIN: Italian
DECK: 2 decks of 52 cards
TIME: 30 minutes
DEGREE OF DIFFICULTY: ☆

Layout

Select one Ace and one King of each suit and place them in a single line. Then deal out the rest of the cards in twelve faceup piles. As you deal the cards onto the piles, play any appropriate card from the stock onto the foundations. *Only* cards from the stock can go onto the foundations during the deal; be sure not to move any from the piles. Don't leave any blanks in the layout as you deal; give a card to each pile. If one card can be played on the foundations, substitute another card for it in the layout.

How to Play

When all the cards have been dealt, start building them up on each other, following suit. Kings may not be put on Aces, nor Aces on Kings. You are allowed two redeals. When gathering up the cards for a redeal, pick them up in reverse sequence from the way you dealt them.

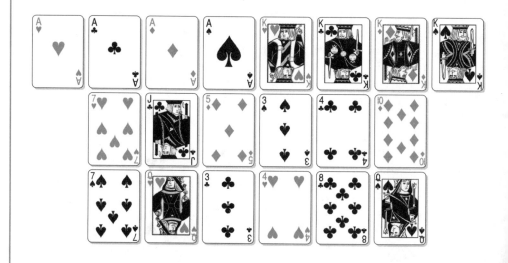

CHAMELEON

ORIGIN: American
DECK: 1 deck of 52 cards
TIME: 10 minutes
DEGREE OF DIFFICULTY: ☆ ☆ ☆

Layout

Deal out a reserve a pile of twelve cards (eleven facedown and the twelfth one faceup). Then place the thirteenth card above the reserve, to be the first foundation; it sets the foundation rank for this deal, and as soon as the others appear place them in the foundation row. Finally, deal a row of three cards to the right of the reserve.

How to Play

Build up on the foundations, following suit, until you form piles of thirteen cards each; Ace goes on the King and below the two. In the three-card row, however, build down in alternating colors. The topmost cards can be moved to the foundations but not to a free space, while sequences can be moved to another pile. Any space that is freed is filled from the the reserve. When the reserve is exhausted, you can refill it from the stock or the wastepile. The cards in the stock are dealt in batches of threes. The topmost card of each group is playable, as well as the ones underneath that become free in the process. The cards that are not playable are placed in a wastepile, the topmost card of which is always available for play. You can redeal the wastepile once.

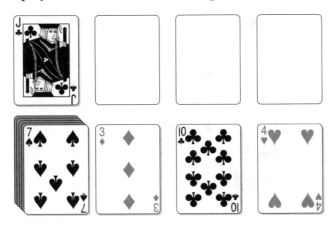

CHESSBOARD

☞ *(Fives)*

ORIGIN: French
DECK: 1 deck of 52 cards
TIME: 15 minutes
DEGREE OF DIFFICULTY: ☆

Layout

Deal all of the cards in piles of three overlapping cards each, in such way that the first row should consist of four piles, the second of three, the third of four, the fourth of three, and the fifth of four; the last pile of which will have only one card.

How to Play

The fully visible card of each pile is playable, as is the second one when the first has been removed, and so on. As soon as each Ace is freed, remove it to the side to become a foundation on top of which you build ascending sequences, following suit. The topmost cards of the piles can be moved to another topmost card according to suit, either in ascending or descending order, depending on the opportunities that arise. You should, however, aim to free cards of the same suit if the higher ranked one is on top of the lower ranked one, otherwise the game will be blocked. Spaces that are freed cannot be filled again. You can only deal once.

A version of this game allows sequences only in descending order on the topmost cards of the piles. In this case, when the game is blocked, you can collect the cards and, either shuffling them or leaving them in the same order, deal again. After the second deal, when the game is again blocked, try to rescue the game with another device—by putting the topmost card of a pile at the bottom of the same pile and thus uncovering a card that can allow the game to continue. This can be done once, for only one pile.

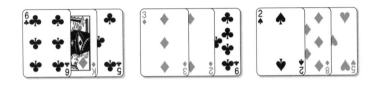

CLIFFS OF DOVER

☞ *(West Cliffs)*

ORIGIN: French
DECK: 1 deck of 52 cards
TIME: 5 minutes
DEGREE OF DIFFICULTY: ☆

Layout

Deal a row of ten piles of four cards each on the tableau. The cards are facedown except for the topmost one of each pile. As you deal, any Aces that show up are placed in a row above the piles. The Aces are the foundations.

How to Play

On top of the foundations, build up to the King, following suit. On the tableau, however, you build down in alternating colors. The topmost card of each pile and the cards facing up from the sequences can be moved, one at a time, to the topmost cards of another pile or to fill free spaces. The topmost cards of the piles can always be placed on the foundations. When there is only one card below the topmost card in one of the piles, you can turn it and use it in the game. The remaining cards of the stock are turned one by one, and are played on the foundations or in the tableau; if they are not usable, place them in a wastepile. The topmost card of the wastepile is always available for play. You are not allowed to redistribute the wastepile.

CLOCK

☞ *(Four of a Kind, Hidden Cards, Hunt, Sundial, Travelers)*

ORIGIN: Russian
DECK: 1 deck of 52 cards
TIME: 5 minutes
DEGREE OF DIFFICULTY: ☆ ☆ ☆

Layout

Deal the cards facedown into thirteen piles of four cards each. Arrange twelve of them in a circle, representing the numbers on a clock dial. Put the thirteenth pile in the middle of the circle as in the layout shown below. The numbers of the clock correspond to the rank of the card each pile represents; one is the Ace, two is the two, and so on, with eleven as the Jack, twelve as the Queen, and the thirteenth pile as the King.

How to Play

Start by turning faceup the topmost card of the thirteenth pile. Then slip it, faceup, under the pile of cards that correspond to its rank. For example, if the turned card is a four of Clubs, it is slid, faceup, under the 4 o'clock pile. Then you turn over the topmost card of the 4 o'clock pile under which you slid the four of Clubs card. Proceed in this manner.

If there are no more cards to turn in that pile, or the uncovered card matches the same pile, turn the card of the next-highest pile. The goal is to form thirteen piles of four cards of the same rank and to finish at the end of the game with the last pile.

To win the game, be sure to get all of the cards turned faceup before the fourth King is turned up.

CLOVER LEAF

ORIGIN: French
DECK: 1 deck of 52 cards
TIME: 15 minutes
DEGREE OF DIFFICULTY: ☆ ☆

Layout

This game is similar to the one of "La Belle Lucie," but differs from it because it is simplified and adapted for players who don't want to get too involved.

Select from the deck the four Aces for the foundations and place them in a row of alternating colors. Deal the remaining cards into fans of three cards each, in four rows with four fans each.

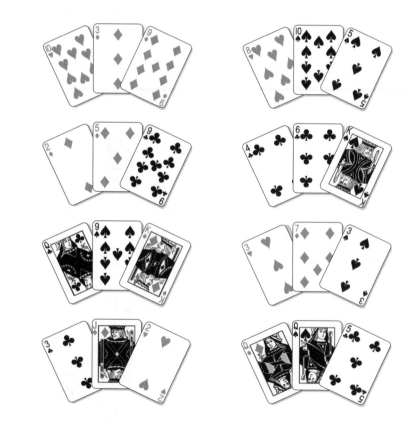

How to Play

The fully visible card of each fan is playable, and the card below becomes playable as soon as the topmost card is moved. The cards are built up on the Aces or used to build down on the topmost card of other sets, following suit. The sequences formed on the fans can be completely moved on top of a card with which it forms a sequence. When the game is blocked, collect the piles and, without shuffling, deal them in the same order as the first deal and then restart the game. Any leftover cards are a set by themselves. You can redeal twice.

After the last deal, when you become blocked again, you get one free move. You can pull one card from underneath one or two others, and play it any way you want, to rescue the game.

COLORADO

ORIGIN: American
DECK: 2 decks of 52 cards
TIME: 15 minutes
DEGREE OF DIFFICULTY: ☆

Layout
Deal two rows of ten cards each on the tableau. When the Aces and Kings, which are the foundations, show up, place them above the tableau: the four Aces at the left and the four Kings at the right, one for each suit.

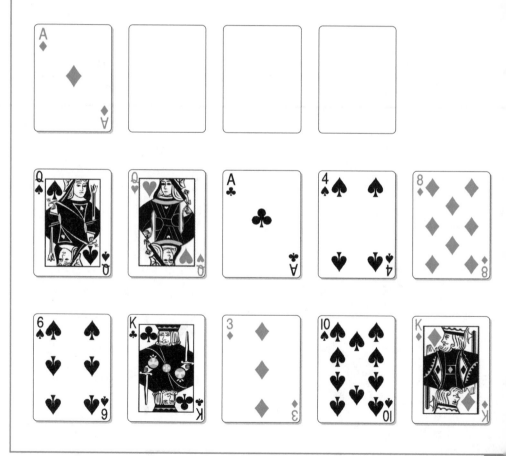

How to Play

Build the Aces up to the King and build the Kings down to the Ace, always following suit. First, play whatever you can to the foundations. As spaces open up in the layout, fill them at once with cards from the stock.

Turn over the cards from the stock one by one, playing them either on the foundations or on top of any of the cards in the tableau; the tableau represents the wastepile, so you can add cards to it without paying attention to the suit or rank. No card can be moved off the tableau, except to be placed on a foundation. The topmost card of each pile in the tableau can be moved to the foundations freely, but only before the next card is drawn from the stock. Thus it is not possible to move the cards of the tableau from one pile to the next. The spaces that become empty are filled, but only with one of the cards from the stock. Dealing again is not permitted.

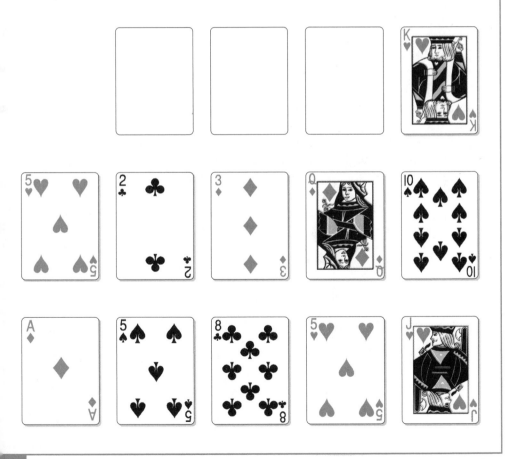

BIG BOOK OF SOLITAIRE ♦

CONGRESS

☞ *(President's Cabinet)*

ORIGIN: American
DECK: 2 decks of 52 cards
TIME: 10 minutes
DEGREE OF DIFFICULTY: ☆ ☆ ☆

Layout

Deal a column of four cards to the left and a column of four cards to the right. Leave enough space between them for the foundations—eight Aces. The cards of the two columns to the right and the left are the tableau. While you are dealing, as soon as the Aces show up place them in the two central columns.

How to Play

Build the Aces up to the Kings, following suit. First, make whatever moves you can to the foundations. Then start turning over the cards of the stock, one by one, building downward on the tableau, regardless of suit and playing whatever cards you can to the foundations. Any cards that are not playable are placed into a wastepile, the topmost card of which is always available for play. You can move only one card at a time from the stock to the foundations or on top of another card of the tableau. Fill in spaces from the wastepile or from the stock.

  You are only allowed to deal once. If you like, you can allow yourself the privilege of looking underneath the topmost card of the wastepile to see if you want to play the card beneath or not; in the case where there is a free space on the tableau, however, you are forced to play this card.

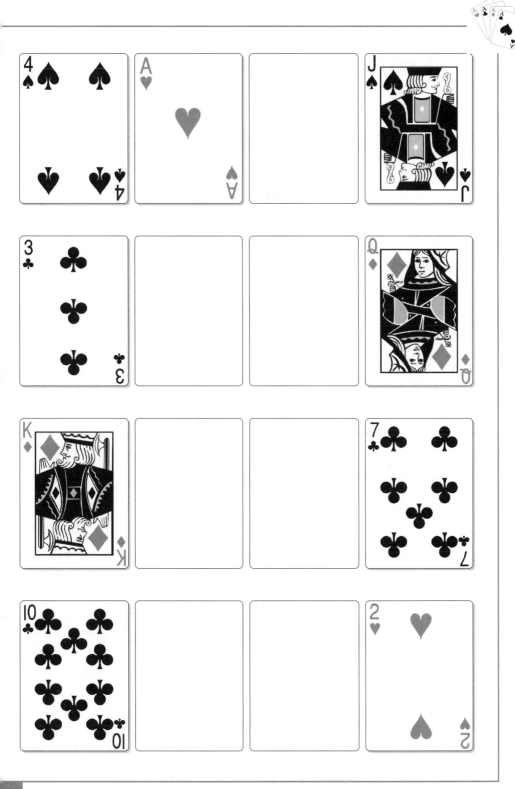

CONSTITUTION

ORIGIN: American
DECK: 2 decks of 52 cards
TIME: 20 minutes
DEGREE OF DIFFICULTY: ☆

Layout

Select the Kings and Queens from the deck and set them aside; they are eliminated. Select all the Aces and place them in one row at the top; they are the foundations. Underneath the row of Aces, deal three rows of eight cards each in the tableau.

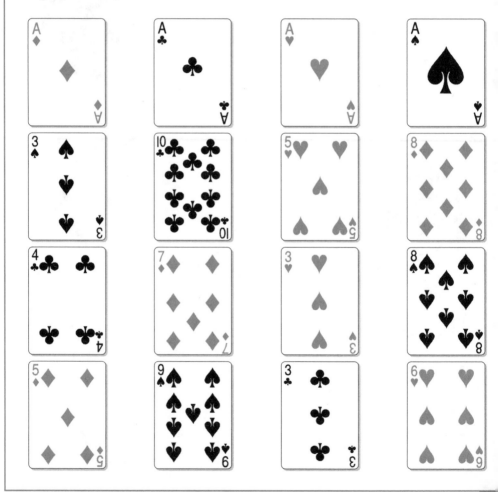

How to Play

Build the foundations up from the Ace to the Jack, following suit. Only the cards of the top row of the tableau can be moved on top of the foundations. You can build descending sequences of alternating colors on the top cards of the top row of the tableau. The cards which can be used for building sequences in the top row of the tableau are the topmost cards in the piles of the upper row, and those that are part of the second row. The topmost card of a sequence cannot be moved to fill a free space. The empty spaces are filled with cards from the bottom row, so that the game is always moving towards the top. The free spaces left in the bottom row of the tableau are only filled with cards from the stock. When the game becomes blocked so that none of the cards of the tableau is playable and you cannot create a space by moving a card, then the game is lost.

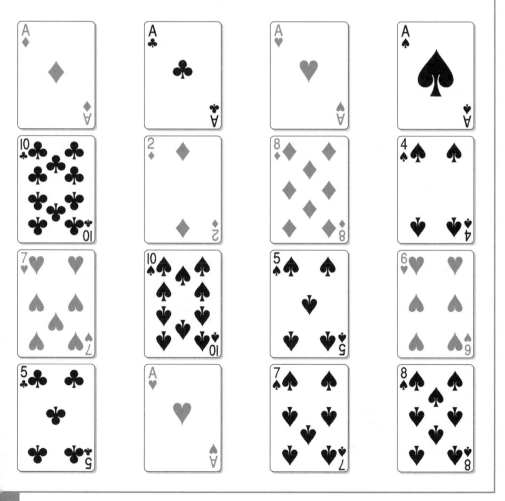

CRAZY QUILT

☞ *(Indian Carpet, Japanese Rug, Tapestry of Baghdad)*

ORIGIN: British
DECK: 2 decks of 52 cards
TIME: 15 minutes
DEGREE OF DIFFICULTY: ☆ ☆ ☆

Layout

Select four Kings and four Aces of different suits and set them out face up; these are the foundations. Our layout below shows two rows, but ordinarily they are placed in one row, the Aces at the left and the Kings at the right. Deal out a reserve or "quilt" of eight rows of eight faceup cards each, laying the cards vertically and horizontally in turn and overlapping each, as shown in the layout opposite.

How to Play

Build the Aces up to the King and build the Kings down to the Ace, always following suit. Any card at the edge of the quilt, displayed vertically, ia available and can be placed to a foundation, and its place will be occupied by the card immediately next to it. In this way, the cards of the quilt are reduced and spaces are not otherwise filled. Turn over the stock one card at a time, placing the card in a wastepile if it cannot be played to a foundation; the topmost card of the wastepile is always available for play. To release a useful card in the quilt, an available card may be played from the quilt to the top of the wastepile in either ascending or descending suit sequence. The stock may be redealt once.

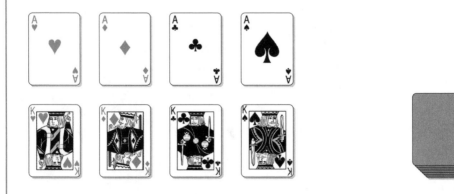

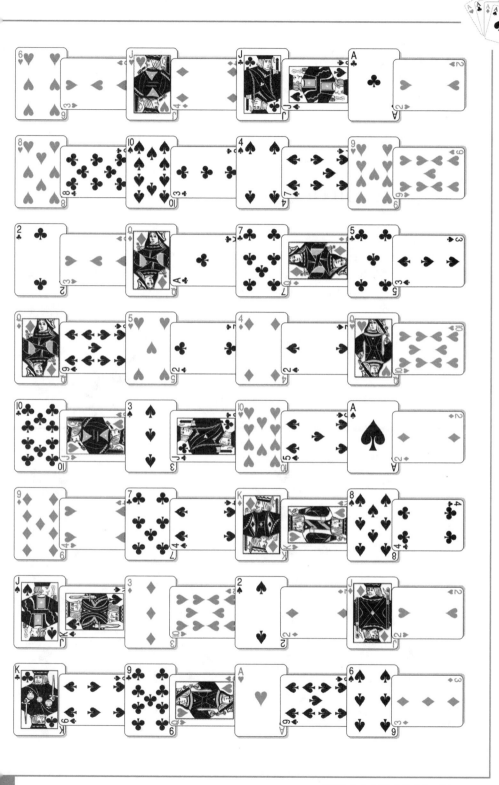

DAUPHIN

☞ *(Stalactite, The Old Groundhog)*

ORIGIN: French
DECK: 1 deck of 52 cards
TIME: 10 minutes
DEGREE OF DIFFICULTY: ☆

Layout

Deal a row of four cards faceup across the top; these are the foundations. In the tableau, deal the remaining cards in eight piles of six cards each, fanned down toward the player, faceup.

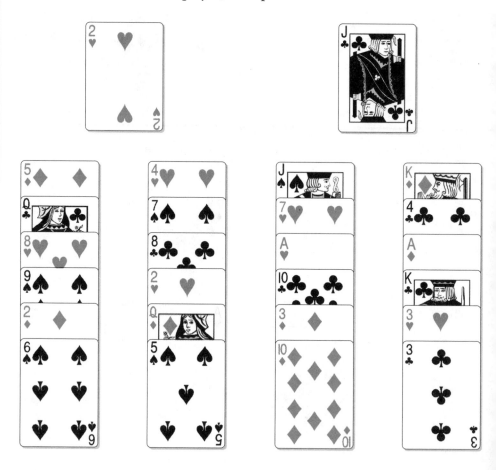

How to Play

First, carefully study the cards and decide for yourself in which way it is best to proceed with building. You can build, regardless of the suits, ascending sequences at intervals of one card (eight, nine, ten, Jack) or of two cards (seven, nine, Jack, King, two, four). Decide for each of the foundations separately whether you will build in intervals of one or two cards. Then start building until each pile has thirteen cards. Only the fully visible card of each pile in the tableau is available for play; however, you also have permission to take up to two cards from any pile, even if they are surrounded by other cards, and set them aside as a "reserve" to tap into when necessary. You are not allowed to fill empty spaces.

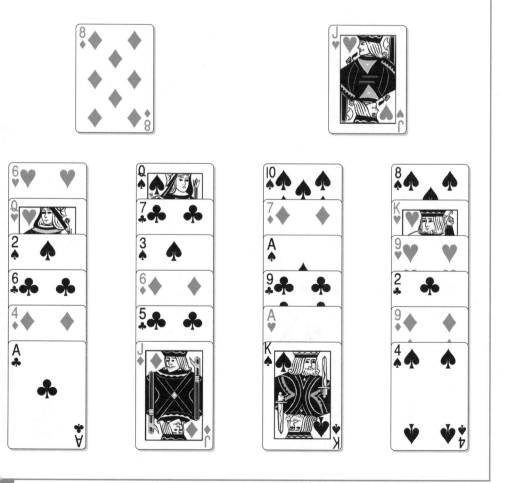

DIPLOMAT

ORIGIN: Austrian
DECK: 2 decks of 52 cards
TIME: 15 minutes
DEGREE OF DIFFICULTY: ☆ ☆

Layout

Deal the cards to form two "wings," with four groups of four cards per side, with the cards overlapping, as shown below. At the center leave enough space to place the eight Aces as soon as they become available.

How to Play

Build the Aces up to the Kings, following suit. The fully visible card of each pile is playable. First make what moves you can to the foundations. Then build descending sequences on the tableau, regardless of suit. Turn the cards of the stock over one by one, playing what you can. Place the unused cards in a wastepile, of which the topmost card is always available for play. Free spaces are filled with cards from the tableau, the stock, or the wastepile. After the stock is exhausted, turn over the wastepile once.

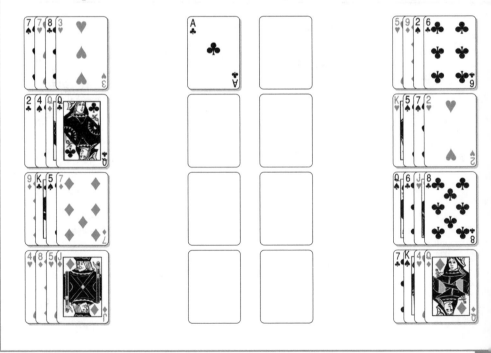

EAGLE WINGS

☞ *(Wings)*

ORIGIN: French
DECK: 1 deck of 52 cards
TIME: 5 minutes
DEGREE OF DIFFICULTY: ☆

Layout

Deal thirteen cards facedown in a squared pile at the center of the tableau; this little pile is called the body. Then lay out four cards, faceup, on one side of the body, and four cards faceup on the other; these form the eagle "wings." Deal one more card, faceup, above the body; this last card is the first foundation. As cards of equal rank to this show up, place them on either side also as foundations.

How to Play

Build up on foundations in ascending order (when you reach the King you continue with the Ace), following suit, full thirteen-card suites. Turn over the cards of the stock one at a time. If you cannot play the card onto a foundation, put it in a wastepile, of which the topmost card is always available for play. You can also play the wing cards to the foundations. Fill spaces in the wings from the facedown body pile. The last card of the body can be turned over and played to the foundations. When the body pile is exhausted, deal another thirteen cards facedown from the stock. Once the stock is exhausted, you can turn the wastepile twice.

EMPEROR

☛ *(Sultan, Kaiser)*

ORIGIN: Austrian
DECK: 2 decks of 52 cards
TIME: 10 minutes
DEGREE OF DIFFICULTY: ☆

Layout

Select from the cards the eight Kings and one Ace of Hearts and place them as shown opposite. Add four cards from the pack on each side of the Kings. You can use these cards to build onto the foundations. All the Kings—and the Ace—are foundations, except for the King of Hearts that is in the middle of the square; don't build on it.

How to Play

Build all the Kings (except the middle King of Hearts) up to the Queens, following suit—and build the Ace of Hearts up to a Queen, also. Of course, to build up the Kings, you're going to need to add an Ace before starting on the twos.

Go through the cards of the stock one by one and start adding to the foundations. Any cards that you can't use go into a wastepile. As soon as a space opens up in the tableau, fill it at once, either from the wastepile of from the stock. Once the stock is exhausted, you are allowed to go through the wastepile twice, shuffling well each time before going through the cards. An enjoyable part of this game is the way it looks when you win.

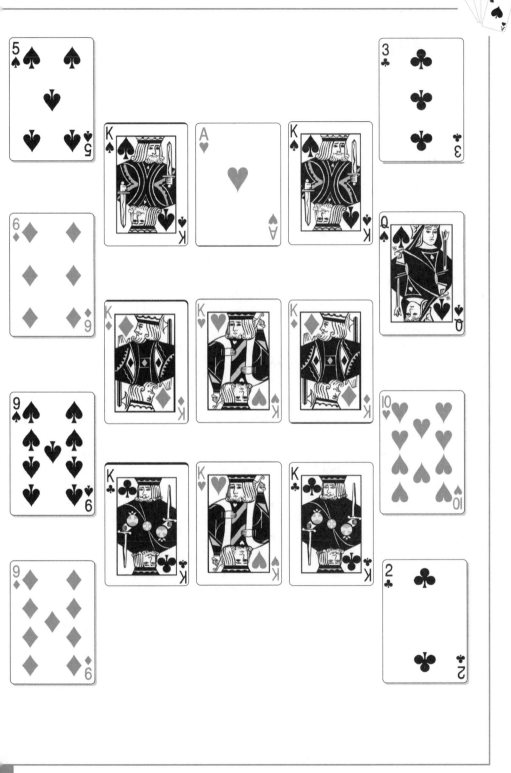

EMPRESS

☞ *(Victoria)*

ORIGIN: British
DECK: 4 decks of 52 cards
TIME: 30 minutes
DEGREE OF DIFFICULTY: ☆ ☆

Layout

Divide the cards at the start into red and black: Diamonds and Hearts, Spades and Clubs. Select from the deck the eight red Aces, the eight black Jacks, and the eight black Kings. You also extract the eight red Queens, but of these you keep only one, the Queen of Hearts, which is placed in the center of the game; the others are eliminated. The Queen of Hearts represents the Empress.

The foundations are the eight red Aces and the eight black Kings, which represent bodyguards to the Empress, placed as shown opposite. Deal four rows of twelve cards each, faceup; the first two rows need to be made with black cards and the other two with red cards.

How to Play

Build up on the Aces and build down on the Kings, always following suit; in the sequences on top of the red Aces you will skip the Queens, jumping from the Jack to the King; and in the sequences on the black Kings you will skip the Jacks. The cards of the four lower rows are reserve cards and will be, as soon as possible, placed on the foundations. Empty spaces in the lower four rows are filled with cards from the wastepile or the stock. The black and red piles of the refuse need to be kept separately. The red and black cards of the lower rows can be connected in alternating descending sequences of red and black. Turn the cards of the stock one at a time and play them to the reserve rows or place them in the wastepiles. The cards of the deck or of the wastepile cannot be replaced directly on the foundations, but must first pass through the lower rows. After the stock is exhausted, you can turn over the wastepiles once.

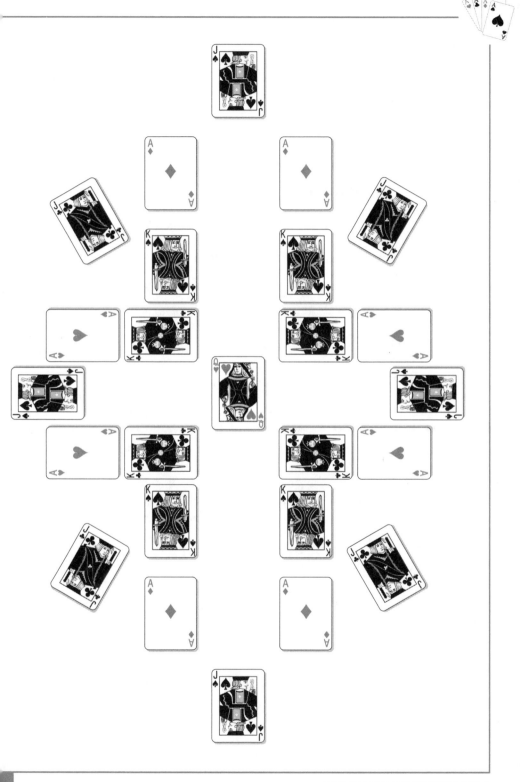

THE FAMILY

ORIGIN: Italian
DECK: 1 deck of 52 cards
TIME: 10-15 minutes
DEGREE OF DIFFICULTY: ☆

Layout

Select the four nines and four tens and place them at the four cardinal points, as shown in the layout opposite; these are foundations.

After placing the the foundation cards, deal the first three cards of the deck in a row underneath the game; these are the available cards, and can be placed on top of the foundations when the opportunity appears. The King, the Queens, and the Jacks are put in their places only for figurative purposes since they have no rank in the game; they are put in their places, shown opposite, as they show up.

How to Play

Build down on the foundations in alternating sequences, following suit. On top of the nine place odd cards: the seven, five, three, and Ace. On top of the ten place even cards: the eight, six, four, and two.

The three available cards can be moved to form ascending sequences on each other, and can always be used to make the sequences on the nines and tens. Turn over the stock one card at a time and play it to the foundations or to the available cards. The cards that are not playable are placed in a wastepile. When a free space appears among the row of available cards, you can fill it either with cards from the deck or with cards from the wastepile, at your convenience. After the stock is exhausted, you can turn the wastepiles over once.

FENCE

ORIGIN: British
DECK: 1 deck of 52 cards
TIME: 10 minutes
DEGREE OF DIFFICULTY: ☆ ☆ ☆

Layout

Deal at the sides of the tableau two columns of five cards each, faceup; these are the reserve. Between the two columns, allow enough space for four cards in a row. Deal two rows of four cards faceup in the middle. As you are dealing, move any Aces that show up to a row at the top; these are the foundations.

How to Play

Build on the foundations up to the King, following suit. The cards of the reserve and of the tableau are playable on the foundations. On the cards of the tableau, you can build down, in alternating colors. You can also move the cards in groups. Turn the stock one card at a time and, if they are not playable, place them in a wastepile, of which the top card is always available for play. Empty spaces in the reserve are filled with cards from the central rows; empty spaces in the central rows are filled with cards from the wastepile, or from the stock if the wastepile is empty. If there are no cards left in the wastepile or the stock, fill the tableau spaces with other cards from the tableau.

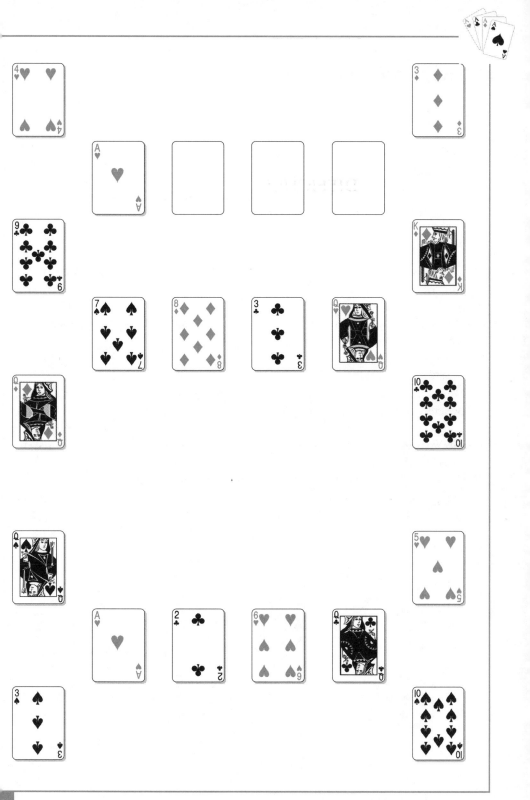

FIRING SQUAD

☞ *(Aces Up, Idiot's Delight)*

ORIGIN: French
DECK: 1 deck of 52 cards
TIME: 10 minutes
DEGREE OF DIFFICULTY: ☆ ☆

Layout

Deal four cards in a row on the table. If you have two cards of the same suit, discard the one that is lower in rank. The Aces have a higher rank than the Kings. For the first row, fill any space from the stock, again eliminating the lower card of the same suit, until you have four cards in a row and can make no more moves.

How to Play

Deal a second row of four cards on the first row. Go through the same process of eliminating the lower card of the same suit from the new layer of cards. Continue in this way until you have exhausted the deck, always discarding inferior cards of the same suit. Fill any space with a card lifted from another pile. It is necessary to weigh the possibilities offered by this type of move before dealing four new cards. The Aces can be placed only in previously free spaces. The spaces are best used to free other cards. Discard all of the cards, except the Aces, which should end up in a row of four.

FLOWERING HILLS

ORIGIN: French
DECK: 1 deck of 52 cards
TIME: 20 minutes
DEGREE OF DIFFICULTY: ☆

Layout
Create six fans of six cards each. Place the remaining sixteen cards on the table or keep them in your hand; these function as a reserve.

How to Play
The fully visible card of each fan is free; build on top of it, in descending sequence, using a free card from the reserve, a free card from another fan, or a descending sequence built on the free card of another fan. As the Aces are freed, they are placed in a column to the right; these are the foundations. Build up on the foundations, following suit. When a fan is exhausted, replace it with a card from the reserve or one or more cards from descending sequence taken from another fan.

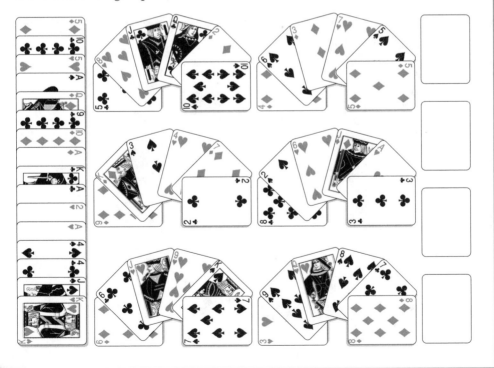

FORTRESS

ORIGIN: French
DECK: 1 deck of 52 cards
TIME: 15 minutes
DEGREE OF DIFFICULTY: ☆ ☆

Layout

Deal twelve cards, forming a square with four cards for each side; these are the walls of the fortress. At the four corners, place the four Aces, which represent the four towers of the fortress; these are the foundations.

How to Play

Build on the foundations up to the King, following suit. The twelve cards are the available cards, and when the occasion shows up you can place them on top of the foundations. You can also form descending sequences that follow suit on any of the cards in the square. Turn the cards of the stock over one at a time, playing them to the square; they cannot go directly to the foundations—that is, they must pass through the walls of the fortress to get to the towers. Unused cards are placed in a wastepile. Fill empty spaces with cards from the stock or from the wastepile. When the stock is exhausted, you can turn the wastepile over once.

FOUR CORNERS

☞ *(Puss in the Corner)*

ORIGIN: British
DECK: 1 deck of 52 cards
TIME: 10 minutes
DEGREE OF DIFFICULTY: ☆ ☆

Layout
Place the four Aces so that they form a square; these are the foundations.

How to Play
Build on the foundations up to the King, regardless of suit but according to color (red on red and black on black). Deal four cards from the stock, placing them diagonal to the Aces, as shown. After dealing the first four cards, play them to the foundations, if possible. Unused cards remain. Deal four more cards to the diagonal locations, again playing them to the foundations after dealing, if possible. In this way you will be creating four wastepiles, keeping in mind that only the topmost card of each is playable. After exhausting the stock by dealing sets of four, pick up the wastepiles and deal four at a time, once through again.

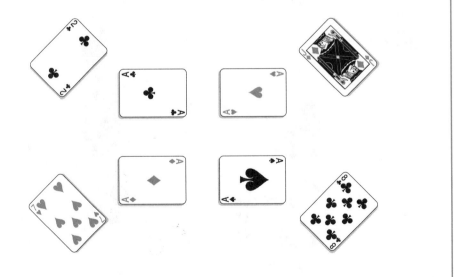

FOUR MEDDLERS

ORIGIN: French
DECK: 2 decks of 52 cards
TIME: 20 minutes
DEGREE OF DIFFICULTY: ☆

Layout

Select the eight Kings and place in pairs in a row; these are the foundations. Deal a column of four cards at the far left below the foundations; these are the available cards. To the right of the first card in the column, deal eight other cards in a row. These, and all rows that follow, are the reserve.

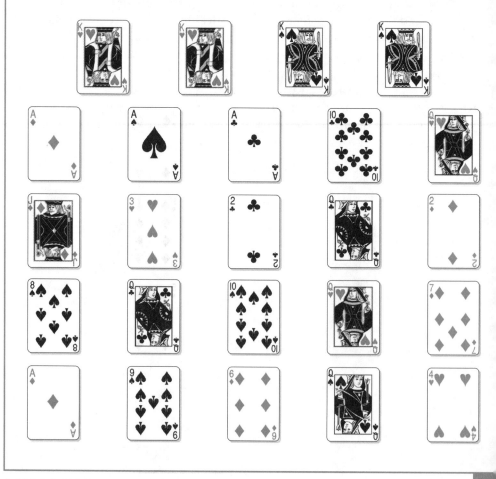

How to Play

Build on the Kings up to the Queens. Play any of the available cards that you can on the foundations. The available cards can also be played on each other in descending sequences. The cards of the reserve can also be placed on the foundations or used to fill empty spaces among the available cards, but they cannot be used to form sequences.

Deal a new row of eight cards; empty spaces created by cards taken from the reserve are not filled. When the game is blocked, deal another row of eight cards. After the last row of eight cards is dealt, four cards called the "meddlers" will remain. These cards are placed in a column at the far right. The meddlers change the game: you can place on the foundations available cards, cards from the reserve, or the four meddlers. If, after having done all possible moves, there is an empty space in the column of meddlers, the game is won.

FOUR TRESPASSERS

ORIGIN: French
DECK: 2 decks of 52 cards
TIME: 15 minutes
DEGREE OF DIFFICULTY: ☆

Layout

Select the eight Aces and place them in a row; these are the foundations. To the left of the Aces place four cards in a column; these are the available cards. Below the Aces place a row of eight cards; these, and all rows that follow, are the reserve.

How to Play

Build on the foundations up to the King, following suit. Cards are played to the foundations first from the available cards and then from the

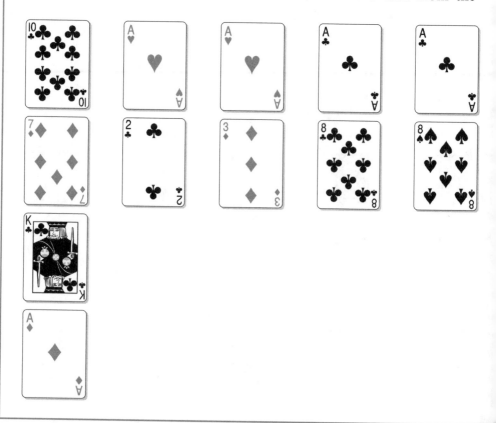

reserve, if the reserve card meets certain conditions—the reserve cards are playable to the foundations if they don't have a card either to the side, above, or below. Thus if a reserve card is at the edge of the tableau, at the bottom of a column, or has an empty space above, below, or to the side, then the reserve card can be played to the foundations. Reserve cards must fill spaces in the available cards, but no spaces are filled in the reserve. You can build descending sequences according to suit on the available cards and on the reserve cards, and an entire pile can be moved as if it were one entity.

When the game is blocked, deal another row of eight cards. After the last row of eight cards is dealt, four cards called the trespassers will remain; these cards are placed in a column at the far right. The trespassers can be played to the foundations or to the reserve, but, just as with the available cards, you always need to fill the empty spaces in this column, so that these cards are always four. Once the trespassers have been put in their places, the cards of the reserve can only be played on top of the trespassers or on the foundations; it is no longer possible to play on the available cards or on the reserve cards. The game is won when the foundations have been built up to the Kings.

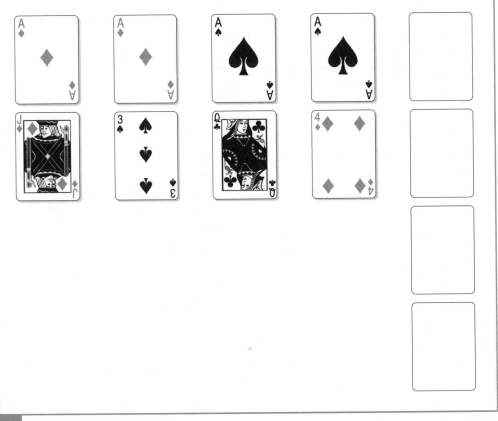

BIG BOOK OF SOLITAIRE ♦

FRIENDSHIP

ORIGIN: Italian
DECK: 1 deck of 52 cards
TIME: 15 minutes
DEGREE OF DIFFICULTY: ☆

Layout

Select the four Aces and place them in a row; these are the foundations. Deal a row of four cards faceup below the row of Aces. The goal of the game is to build the foundations from Ace up to the King.

How to Play

Use the cards from the row beneath the Aces to build the foundations up to the King, following suit, or to form descending columns of alternating colors on top of these cards. If, for example, you have dealt a card that you can place on the foundations, you proceed with this operation; if, among the dealt cards, there is one that can be placed in descending sequence on top of another card, you proceed with this move. As a place occupied by one of the first four cards becomes free, fill it immediately by dealing the topmost card from the stock.

Once you have finished these operations and the game has become blocked, deal four more cards from the stock below the first row of four. With these four new cards you can build on the foundations or continue to form descending columns of alternating colors on top of first row of four. Again, if an empty space becomes available in the first row, fill it immediately with one of the new cards or by dealing the topmost card from the stock. Once you have finished all possible moves with this new series of four cards, you need to place the unused new cards in a wastepile. The topmost card of the wastepile is always available for play. Proceed by dealing another bottom row of four cards, playing in the same manner until the stock is exhausted. The wastepile can then be turned over once, also by dealing four cards at a time.

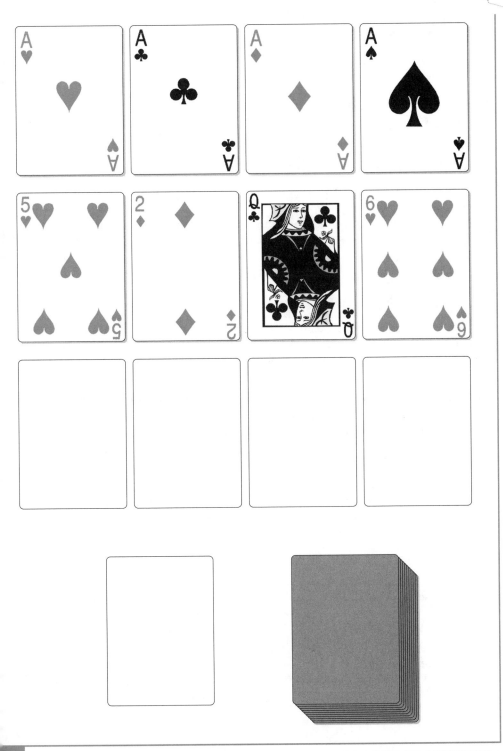

THE GARDEN

☞ *(Italian Flower Garden, February 1865)*

ORIGIN: Italian
DECK: 1 deck of 52 cards
TIME: 20 minutes
DEGREE OF DIFFICULTY: ☆

Layout

Deal six columns of six overlapping cardseach; this is the "garden." Spread the remaining sixteen cards out in front of you in a fan; these cards are the "bouquet" or reserve. (Two fans are shown in the diagram opposite because of space constraints.)

How to Play

When the Aces become playable, move them to form a column at the right or a row at the top of the game; these are the foundations. Build on the Aces up to the King, following suit. Start building on the exposed cards at the bottom of the columns, one card at a time, and on the foundations. The exposed cards of the columns can be built down regardless of suit. If a space becomes freed, fill it with any available card. Every card of the bouquet is available for building at all times.

In order for this solitaire to be successful, we advise you to build as little as possible with the cards of the bouquet, which are most useful for moving cards to the foundations. Also, in order to build easily, make sure you first free the lowest ranking cards in the columns of the garden.

Did you know?

The origin of this game is associated with the transfer of the court of Victor Emmanuel II (1820-1878) from Turin to Florence, the new capital of the united Italian Kingdom. It is said that during his travels the King passed some of the time having his knights teach him card games.

GARGANTUA

☞ *(Rabelais)*

ORIGIN: French
DECK: 2 decks of 52 cards
TIME: 20 minutes
DEGREE OF DIFFICULTY: ☆

Layout

Deal on the tableau nine piles of cards, the first consisting of one card, the second of two, the third of three, and so on until you have the final pile of nine cards. The topmost card of each pile should be faceup while the ones underneath should be facedown. As soon as the Aces become playable, place them in a row at the top or the bottom of the tableau; these are the foundations.

How to Play

Build on the foundations up to the Kings, following suit. On top of the nine piles, however, you can build down in alternating colors. The columns you manage to build can be moved as a whole or in part on top of another pile, if that pile has a faceup card that allows you to continue the sequence. Once the top card is played, you can turn the one underneath faceup and it automatically becomes usable. When the game is blocked, collect the cards from the piles, shuffle them well, and redeal them into nine piles as explained at the beginning. You are permitted to redeal only once.

THE GATE

ORIGIN: Italian
DECK: 1 deck of 52 cards
TIME: 15 minutes
DEGREE OF DIFFICULTY: ☆

Layout

Deal thirteen cards faceup, as the layout opposite shows, in the shape of
an arch; four cards on either side of five cards arched across the top.
During the deal, whenever a Jack shows up, place it in a row at the
bottom of the arch to form the gate; these are the foundations.

How to Play

Build onto the foundations following suit in descending sequences—ten,
nine, eight, through the Ace and King to the Queen. After dealing the
thirteen cards of the arch, deal a pile of five cards, four facedown and the
topmost faceup; these are the reserve. Play any cards of the arch, or the
topmost reserve card to the foundations.

Look over the cards that form the arch, and if among these there are
two of the same rank, remove one of them and place it in the reserve pile.
When there are several pairs, remove one card of the pair with the higher
rank and place it at the bottom of the reserve pile. The free spaces can be
filled either with cards from the stock or with cards from the reserve. If
there are three or four equal cards, even if they are of a lower rank
compared to another pair, remove two to the reserve pile.

When you remove the cards from the arch of the gate, we advise you
to leave the cards of the same suit in their place: at the right moment
these can be played to the foundations all together, leaving many empty
spaces for the cards from the reserve or stock.

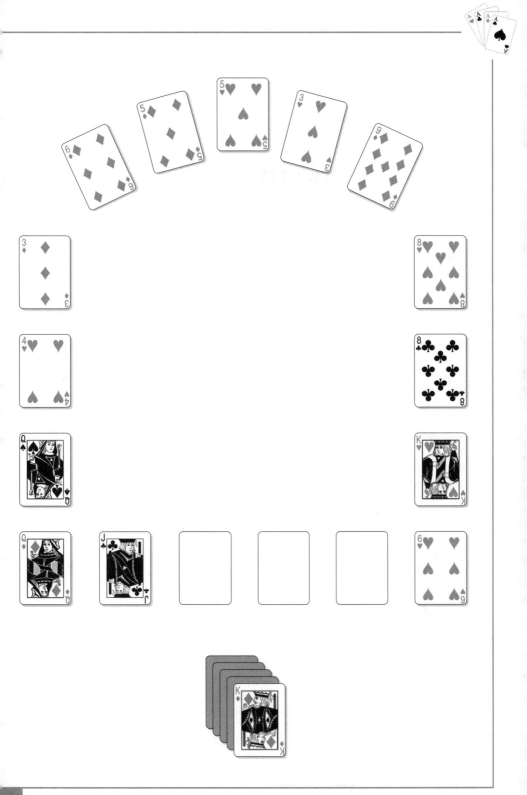

GOLF

ORIGIN: British
DECK: 1 deck of 52 cards
TIME: 5 minutes
DEGREE OF DIFFICULTY: ☆ ☆ ☆

Layout

Deal seven columns of five cards each, overlapping as shown below, as the tableau. Deal one card below the tableau that will start the wastepile. The goal is to get rid of the entire tableau by building up and down on the wastepile, regardless of suit.

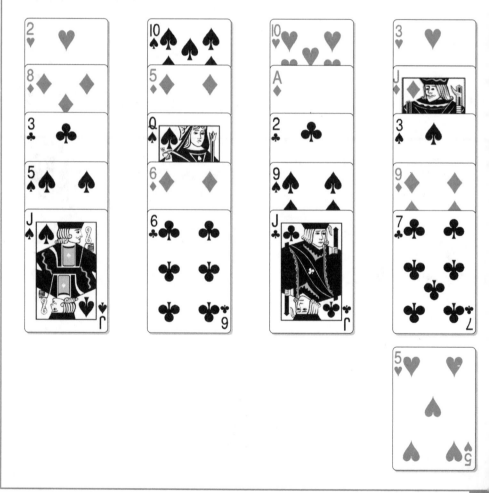

How to Play

Only the exposed cards of the layout are available for building. You cannot build anything on a King. When you put a King on the wastepile, you've ended the sequence. Whenever you end a sequence—by putting down a King or not being able to make another move—you can take a card from the stockpile of sixteen cards that never got into the layout (shown below facedown next to the layout). Place the card from the stock on the wastepile and resume building. When you have used up all the cards from the stock and play is blocked, that "hole" of the golf game is over. Your number of strokes for that "hole" is the number of cards left in the layout, regardless of their rank. The game is repeated nine times to have the total score for a game of golf with nine holes. A good score for nine holes is forty, but achieving this score is very difficult. If the tableau is cleared, then you did better than a hole in one—you had no strokes.

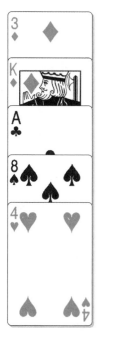

GRANDFATHER'S CLOCK

ORIGIN: Russian
DECK: 1 deck of 52 cards
TIME: 10 minutes
DEGREE OF DIFFICULTY: ☆ ☆

Layout

Select from the deck: two of Hearts, three of Spades, four of Diamonds, five of Clubs, six of Hearts, seven of Spades, eight of Diamonds, nine of Clubs, ten of Hearts, Jack of Spades, Queen of Diamonds, King of Clubs, and display them faceup as shown in the layout below; these are the foundations up on which you are going to be building a "real" clock face. Deal the remaining cards faceup in eight columns of five cards each.

How to Play

Using the exposed cards, build the foundations—the cards of the clock face—up in suit until the cards on the top correspond to the numbers of a real clockface (with Jack as 11 o'clock, Queen as 12, Ace as 1, etc.). In order to free cards to do this, build the exposed cards of the columns downward, regardless of suit. Spaces may be filled by any available card.

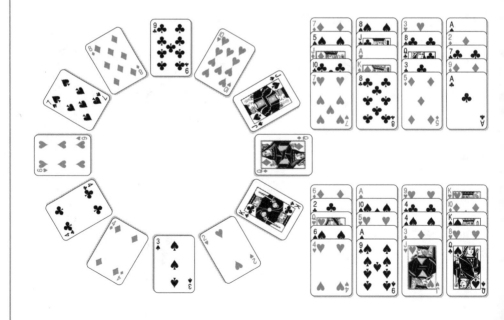

GRAND MAGNOLIA

☞ *(Blooming Tree, Fish Bone)*

ORIGIN: Italian
DECK: 2 decks of 52 cards
TIME: 15 minutes
DEGREE OF DIFFICULTY: ☆

Layout

Deal six cards in two rows of three cards each. When the Aces show up, place them in a column of alternating colors, one underneath the other. The Queens should be tucked under the left side of the Ace of the same suit and the Kings under the right; both positioned only when the Ace of that suit is already in place.

How to Play

Build ascending sequences on top of the Aces up to the Jacks, following suit. Build the sequences with the cards from the rows. Fill spaces in the rows with cards from the stock or with the topmost card from the wastepile. When there are no more moves from the two rows, place those cards in the wastepile and deal two new rows of three cards each. The wastepile can be dealt once. The final figure looks like a fish bone with the backbone formed by Jacks.

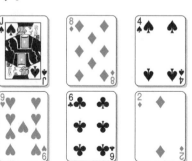

GRANDMA'S SOLITAIRE

ORIGIN: Italian
DECK: 2 decks of 52 cards
TIME: 25 minutes
DEGREE OF DIFFICULTY: ☆ ☆

Layout

Deal 13 piles of face up cards in three rows in the tableau—two rows of five piles and one row of three piles. Deal one card, on each tableau pile. When the Aces and Kings show up, they are placed above in eight foundation piles. The tableau piles are referred to by the ranks of cards:

the first tableau is the Ace pile, the second is the two pile, and so on up to the 13th, which is the King pile. As you deal the tableaus, you will occasionally also deal a card facedown onto a reserve pile. Do this whenever: (1) a card dealt to the tableau is an Ace or a King; (2) the card dealt is at the end of a row; (3) the card's rank matches the pile's name.

How to Play

Build the Aces up and the Kings down, following suit; sequences can be moved from one foundation to another. The topmost cards of the 13 tableau piles are open for play; the piles should be squared so cards underneath are hidden. You can draw a card from the top of the reserve pile at any time. Place this card on the pile it corresponds to and pick up that pile. Fan the pile, playing any cards you can. You cannot draw another card from the reserve until you place this pile back, squared.

GREEK CROSS

ORIGIN: Italian
DECK: 2 decks of 52 cards
TIME: 20-25 minutes
DEGREE OF DIFFICULTY: ☆ ☆

Layout
Of all the more or less geometrical forms given to solitaires, the ones that are most common are the crosses, for the reason that they offer a practical distribution of the cards. Deal eighteen cards in the shape of a cross, eight in the central column and the remaining ones, as shown opposite, in the arms of the cross. Select four Kings from the deck, one for each suit, and arrange them in the following order: the King of Diamonds at the top of the cross, the King of Hearts at the bottom, the King of Spades at the left, and the King of Clubs at the right; these are the foundations.

How to Play
On top of the Kings of Diamonds, Clubs, and Spades, build ascending sequences up to the Queen, following suit. With the King of Hearts, however, build descending sequences to the Ace. On top of the three Kings of Diamonds, Clubs, and Spades you can form only one sequence of the same suit, while the other five sequences will be formed on top of the King of Hearts, regardless of the suit. Since there are only two cards for each suit and each rank, you will need to remember the cards that are placed in the sequence on top of the King of Hearts in order not to find yourself blocked on one of the other Kings. The free spaces that are created in the arms or the central column of the cross can be filled either with cards from the stock or with the topmost card from the wastepile. Stock is turned over one card at a time, and cards that are not playable are placed in the wastepile. The game is successful when all the Aces have found their place on the Kings.

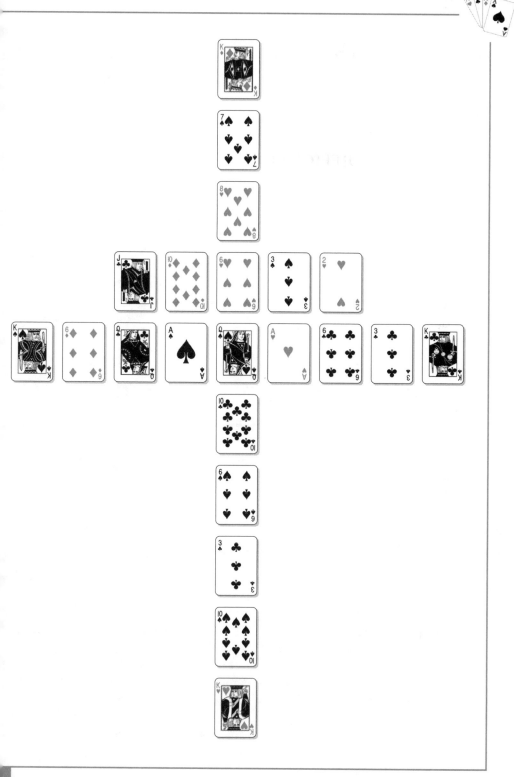

KLONDIKE

☞ *(Fascination, Demon Patience, Small Triangle, Triangle)*

ORIGIN: American
DECK: 1 deck of 52 cards
TIME: 10 minutes
DEGREE OF DIFFICULTY: ☆ ☆

Layout

Deal seven cards in a row—facedown except for the first card. Then put the eighth card faceup on the second card in the row and complete the row with facedown cards. Place a faceup card on the third pile, and finish off the row in the same way. Continue until you have a faceup card on every pile. Each time an Ace appears faceup, place it in a row at the top of the game; these are the foundations.

How to Play

Build up complete suites on the Aces from Ace to King, following suit. Look over the spread carefully and move any cards you can to the foundations. On the tableau you can build on the faceup cards, building down in alternating colors. Every time you move a faceup card, you need to turn up the facedown card beneath it. When there are no more facedown cards in a pile, and you move the faceup card, you can fill the space with any available King.

When you've made all the moves you can, start going through the stock one by one, looking for more cards to build on the foundations and the tableau. If you can't place the card, it goes faceup onto a wastepile, the topmost card of which is always available for play.

Scoring for Klondike is traditionally done in rounds of five games. Add up the number of foundation cards you've come up with in each round for your final score.

Some players prefer to go through the stock by threes—three cards at a time. The advantage is that then you are allowed to redeal, but rules vary as to how many redeals you get. Some say two redeals (three trips through the cards) and some say as many as you want or until there are seven cards in the wastepile, at which point you go through one by one. This game is popular throughout the world because of the combination of judgment, chance, attractive layout, and fast-paced action.

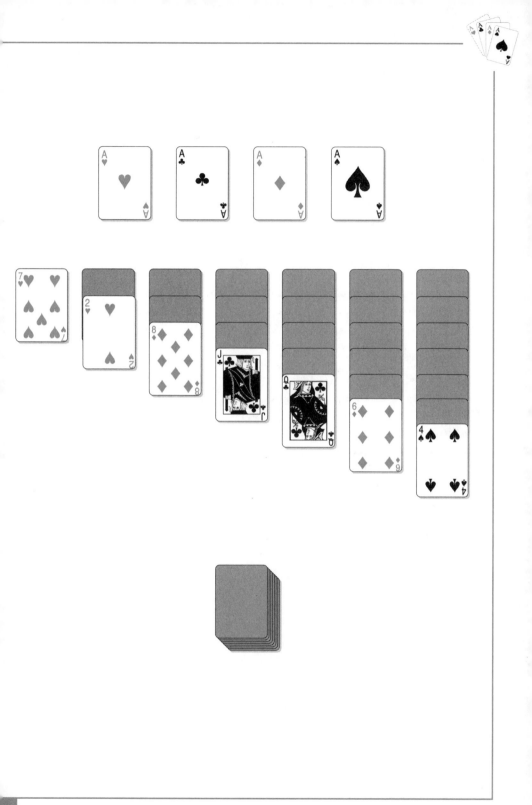

LA BELLE LUCIE

☞ *(Alexander the Great, Fair Lucy, The Fan, Midnight Oil)*

ORIGIN: French
DECK: 1 deck of 52 cards
TIME: 15 minutes
DEGREE OF DIFFICULTY: ☆ ☆

Layout

Deal the entire deck in fans of three, faceup. There will be seventeen fans and one lone card, which becomes its own set. The foundations are the Aces, and they are set out in a row above the tableau as they come into play.

How to Play

Only the fully exposed cards may be moved. Build the foundations up to the King, following suit. One card at a time can be moved to the foundations, or used to build down on another topmost card, also following suit. The sequences on the fans can be moved in their entirety or in part to other topmost cards of the tableau. When a fan is entirely eliminated it is not replaced. When the game becomes blocked, you can gather up the fans, shuffle, and deal fans in groups of three as before. Any leftover cards are sets by themselves. You are allowed to gather up the fans and redeal twice.

In the last redeal, when the game is blocked again, you get one free move—one card you can pull from underneath and play any way that you want.

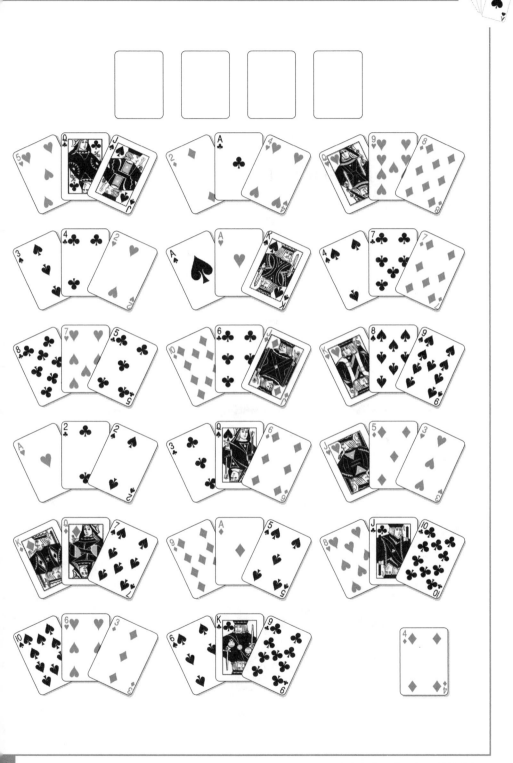

LA ROCHELLE

☛ *(Holes)*

ORIGIN: French
DECK: 1 deck of 52 cards
TIME: 10 minutes
DEGREE OF DIFFICULTY: ☆ ☆

Layout

Deal four rows of thirteen cards faceup. Then remove the Aces and set them aside: this way you will have four empty spaces.

How to Play

Into each space that has been freed by the Aces place a card of higher rank and the same suit as the one to the left of the empty space. For

example, if to the left of the empty space there is a five of Hearts, into the empty space you will place the six of Hearts. The sequences end with the King: no card can be placed in the empty space to the right of the King. As empty spaces occur at the far left, place the twos there. Fill the empty spaces that occur, unless play is blocked by a King.

When the game is blocked, collect the cards of the tableau which are not yet in proper sequence to the right of their two. Shuffle the cards and redeal them in the rows, allowing an empty space to the right of the last card in proper sequence. For example, if the fourth card of the first row is the four of Hearts, and this is the last of the Hearts which have already been placed in order, leave an empty space before dealing the cards back into that row. The cards can be collected and redealt twice. The game is successful when in the rows are sequenced from twos to Kings.

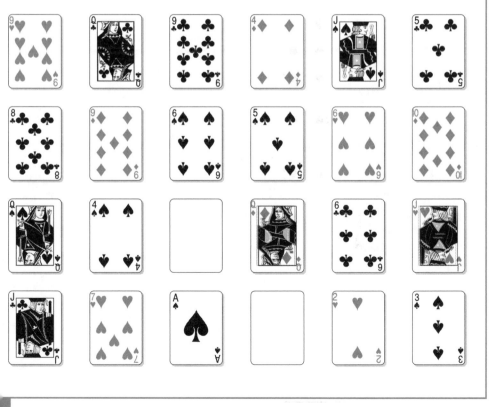

LITTLE SPIDER

ORIGIN: Russian
DECK: 1 deck of 52 cards
TIME: 20 minutes
DEGREE OF DIFFICULTY: ☆ ☆ ☆

Layout
Deal four cards in a row, allow room for a row below this row, and then deal another row of four cards. The empty row will be the foundations, which should be two Aces of one color and two Kings of the other color. In the example opposite, we have two black Aces and two red Kings. Place the foundation cards as they become available.

How to Play
Build the Aces up to the Kings and the Kings down to the Aces, always following suit. There are special rules until all of the cards of the stock have been dealt: You can move any card from the top row onto the foundations, but you can only move the card that is directly below a foundation card straight up onto that foundation pile. Spaces cannot be filled.

When you have made all the moves you can to the foundation piles, deal another four cards to the top row and another four to the bottom row. Make the moves you can and then deal again—until all the cards of the stock have been laid out.

At this point the special rules no longer apply. you can move any card from the top of bottom rows to the foundation piles. now you can also build on the topmost cards of the top and bottom rows with other topmost cards—regardless of suit or color—up or down. Kings may be placed on Aces and Aces on Kings. Building as much as possible on the top and bottom rows will make it easier to eventually transfer all the cards to the foundation piles.

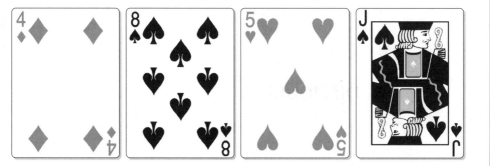

MARY STUART

☞ *(Tapestry)*

ORIGIN: British
DECK: 1 deck of 52 cards
TIME: 5 minutes
DEGREE OF DIFFICULTY: ☆

Layout

Select from the deck the four Aces and you display them in a row at the foundation of the tableau. The Aces are the foundations on top of which you build ascending sequences up to the King, according to suit. Above the foundations you display four rows of cards, each of which ares a reserve.

How to Play

You deal the cards of the deck one by one; the cards that are not playable will be placed in a wastepile, of which the last card is always playable. You can use all cards of the reserve and fill the empty spaces with cards from the deck or from the wastepile. You are not allowed to redistribute.

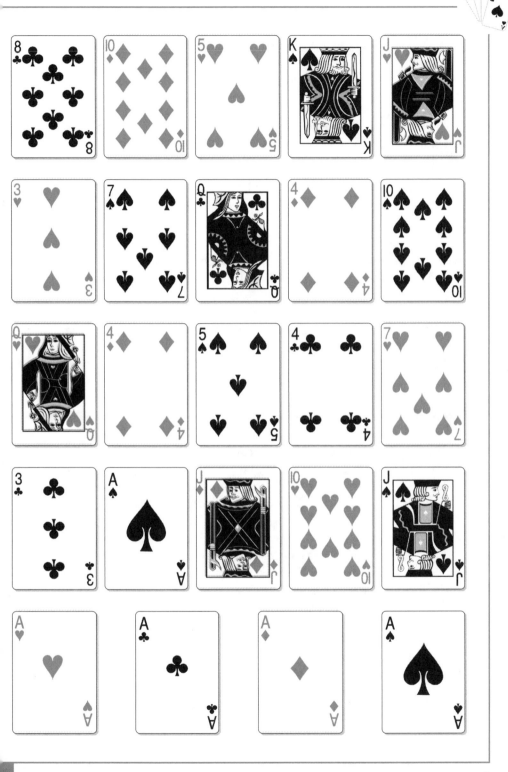

MATRIMONY

☞ *(Wedding)*

ORIGIN: British
DECK: 2 decks of 52 cards
TIME: 15 minutes
DEGREE OF DIFFICULTY: ☆ ☆ ☆

Layout

Select the Jack and the Queen of Hearts, and place them at the top center of the game, the Jack at the right and the Queen at the left. Underneath this couple, allow for another row and then deal two rows of eight cards each; these are the available cards. When the two Jacks of Diamonds show up during the deal, place one above and one below the couple of Hearts. When the two tens of Spades show up, place the to either side of the upper Jack of Diamonds. When the two tens of Clubs show up, place them to either side of the lower Jack of Diamonds. The eight cards in the top three rows are the foundations.

How to Play

Build sequences on the foundations in the following order:

Build up on the Queen of Hearts, following suit: King, Ace, two, three, etc. and finishing with the Jack.

Build down on the three Jacks, following suit: ten, nine, eight, etc. through the King to the Queen, which is the final card.

Build down on the four tens, following suit: ten, nine, eight, etc. through the Ace, King, Queen, and Jack, which is the final card.

Use the available cards to build on the foundations. After making what moves you can, deal another sixteen cards from the stock, covering the ones left over or filling a space, but always so there are sixteen new cards to play. Repeat this process until you have exhausted all the cards of the stock, after which you can pick up the sixteenth pile and use its cards to fill empty spaces. Then deal the remaining cards on the fifteen other piles. Then, in the same way, pick up the fifteenth pile, then the fourteenth, and so on. If the game is successful, you will see at the center a couple surrounded by ladies and pages.

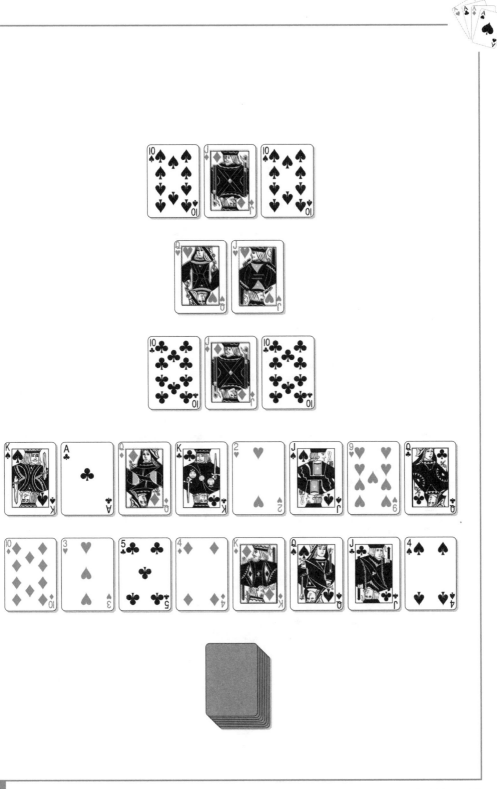

MERIDIAN OF VIENNA

ORIGIN: Austrian
DECK: 2 decks of 52 cards
TIME: 15-20 minutes
DEGREE OF DIFFICULTY: ☆

Layout

Select an Ace and a King for each suit; these will be the foundations. Place them in two columns far enough apart so that four fans of six cards each can be dealt on either side of each column. The sixteen fans should have the cards facedown, except for the topmost one.

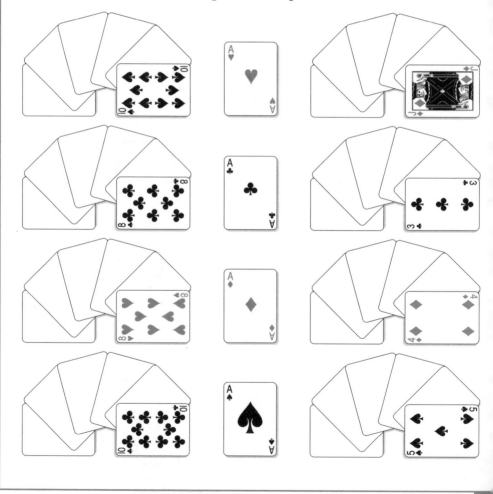

How to Play

Build the Aces up to the Kings, and build the Kings down to the Aces, following suit. The sequence is continual; for example, an Ace can go on a King, and a King on an Ace.

Move the cards one at a time from the fans to the foundations, turning up the card underneath the one removed. Empty spaces that are created by eliminating a fan are not filled. The sequences on the foundations can be moved from one foundation pile to another and turned around in order, according to the needs of the game; Kings and Aces, however, cannot be moved.

When the game is blocked, you can pull out the last card from each fan and place it faceup on topmost card of its fan; this operation can be repeated three times.

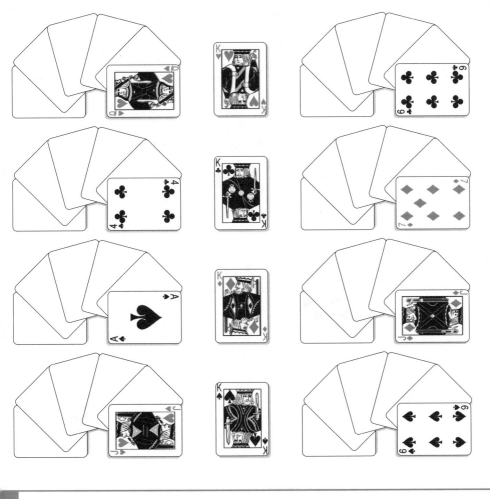

MERMAIDS

ORIGIN: Italian
DECK: 1 deck of 52 cards
TIME: 5 minutes
DEGREE OF DIFFICULTY: ☆

Layout

Eliminate the Kings from the deck. Deal a row of four cards and, as the Aces show up, place them in a row above. The Aces are the foundations.

How to Play

Build on the Aces up to the Queens, following suit. The playable cards are the topmost cards of what will become four piles below the Aces; only the card that is directly below an Ace, however, can be played to that Ace. No sequences can be made on the lower row. After making the moves you can with the first four cards, deal four more cards in the bottom row, covering any that remain or placing them in a space, so that there are four new cards in the row. Empty spaces cannot be filled except in their turn as a layer of four cards is dealt. Make what moves you can and then continue through the stock in the same manner.

After the first deal, all the Aces will be in their places; pick up the cards of the four piles from the right to left, placing them one on top of the other without changing their order. The cards can be picked up and dealt again as long as you have made two moves. If after dealing you have not been able to make two moves, then the game is blocked. When a foundation pile has been completed to its Queen, the pile is eliminated, and the next deal will be made with only three piles, and so on.

METHUSELAH

☞ *(Accordion, Idle Year, Tower of Babel, Tower of London)*

ORIGIN: British
DECK: 1 deck of 52 cards
TIME: 5 minutes
DEGREE OF DIFFICULTY: ☆ ☆ ☆

Layout

Deal all the cards one by one, faceup, into thirteen piles of four cards each. If space allows, place the piles in one row; otherwise treat them as if they were a continuous row from left to right.

How to Play

You play the cards by moving one onto a card it matches in suit or rank—but only at specific locations. Any card may be moved onto the card immediately to its left or onto the third card to its left, as long as they are of the same suit or rank. Two or more cards that have been matched in this way can be moved as a pile, but only the topmost card is considered in making a match. If a card matches both its neighbor and the third to the left, you can choose either one. You win when the cards end up in one pile, but ending with five piles is considered doing well.

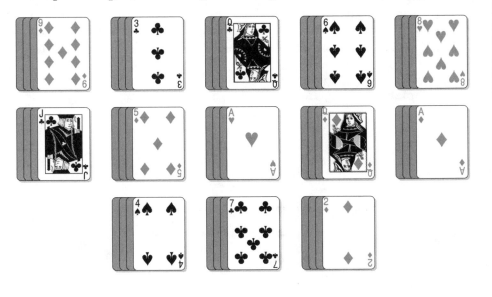

MISS MILLIGAN

ORIGIN: British
DECK: 2 decks of 52 cards
TIME: 20 minutes
DEGREE OF DIFFICULTY: ☆ ☆ ☆

Layout
Deal eight cards faceup in a row. When the Aces show up, place them above in a row as foundations.

How to Play
Build up on the Aces to the Kings, following suit. Build down on the tableau cards in alternating colors. Make what moves you can, and then deal another eight cards overlapping the remaining cards. Move what cards you can to the foundations and build on the columns. Several cards can be transferred together from one column to another if they are in alternating color sequence. Empty spaces may be filled with any available King or with a sequence that leads off with a King, as in our example.

Weaving
When the stock is exhausted, you can "weave," which is the option of removing one card from the bottom row temporarily while you make other moves. When you put the removed card back into play—either on a foundation or in the tableau—you are then allowed to remove another card. You can keep doing this "weaving" until you win the game or until you cannot find a place for the card.

Start of play

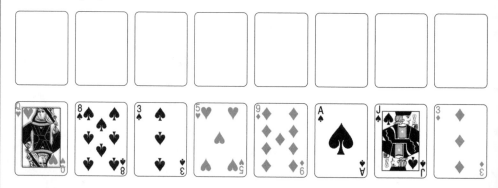

After first moves

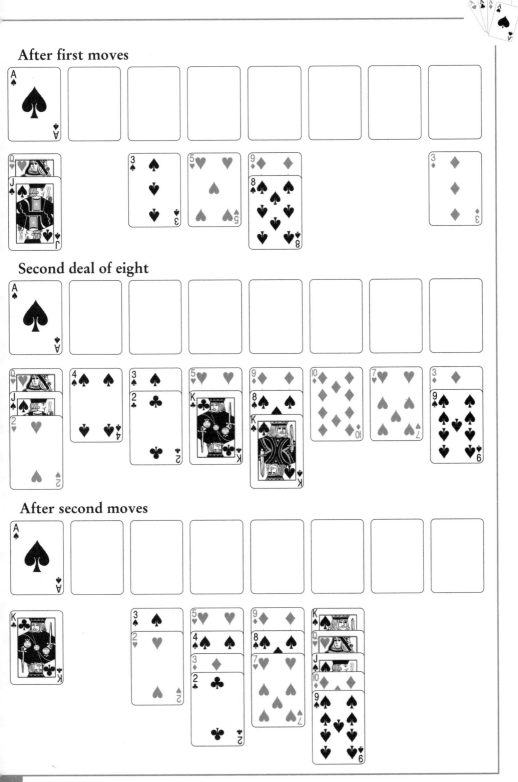

Second deal of eight

After second moves

MONTE CARLO
☞ *(Double and Quits, Weddings)*

ORIGIN: French
DECK: 1 deck of 52 cards
TIME: 10-15 minutes
DEGREE OF DIFFICULTY: ☆ ☆

Layout
Deal five rows of five cards each.

How to Play
Remove the cards in pairs of the same rank if they are adjacent (side to side, top to bottom, or corner to corner). Then close up the cards from right to left, starting at the top row and moving up a card from the left of the next row as needed, preserving the order as originally laid out. Deal new cards at the bottom, so that you have five rows of five cards again. Repeat this until you exhaust the deck or pairing is impossible.

MOUNT OLYMPUS

ORIGIN: Belgian
DECK: 2 decks of 52 cards
TIME: 15 minutes
DEGREE OF DIFFICULTY: ☆

Layout

Select the Aces and twos of each suit and place them in two rows (or, if you want the classic Mount Olympus shape, arrange them in a sweeping arch); these are the foundations. Deal a row of nine cards at the bottom, or go with the mountain shape by placing them in three rows of one card, three cards, and five cards. The shape doesn't change the game; the straight rows are just easier to play on when building sequences.

How to Play

Build on the foundations, following suit but skipping cards in succession in this pattern: Ace, three, five, seven, nine, Jack, King; two four, six, eight, ten, Queen. The cards of the tableau can be placed on top of each other following suit in descending sequences that also skip: King, Jack, nine, seven, five; or ten, eight, six, four, etc. All cards of a pile in sequence can be moved as a unit. Fill empty spaces at once from the stock. Once you have made the moves you can, deal nine more cards onto the tableau. Continue in this way until the stock is exhausted. You are not allowed to redeal.

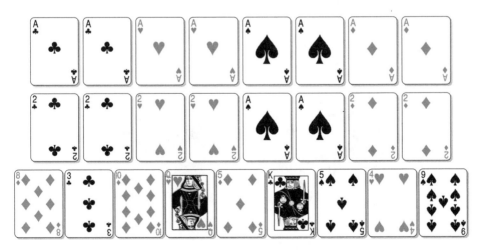

THE MUSES

ORIGIN: Italian
DECK: 1 deck of 52 cards
TIME: 15-20 minutes
DEGREE OF DIFFICULTY: ☆

Layout

Deal the cards in the shape of a triangle starting with a row of nine cards, then underneath this a row of eight cards, and so on until the last row has only one card. Place the remaining seven cards of the deck in a row at the base of the game; they are the reserve (in our layout, they are at the side, because of space considerations).

How to Play

The playable cards are the last ones at bottom of each column and the seven of the reserve. When the Aces are playable, they are moved to a row below the reserve; these are foundations on which you build up to the King, following suit. You can build descending sequences of alternating colors on the playable cards; the cards can be moved only once. Fill a space in the reserve with a card from the bottom of one of the columns. You are not allowed to redeal.

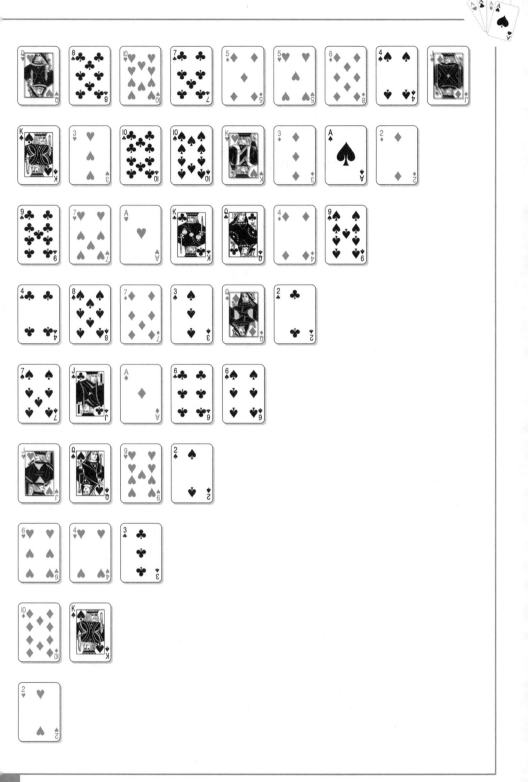

NAPOLEON AT SAINT HELENA

☞ *(A Hundred Days, Cadran, Forty Thieves, Island of Elba)*

ORIGIN: French
DECK: 2 decks of 52 cards
TIME: 20-25 minutes
DEGREE OF DIFFICULTY: ☆ ☆

Layout

Deal four rows of ten cards each, overlapping as shown in the layout below. As the Aces become available, they are moved above the tableau as the foundations.

How to Play

Build the foundations up to Kings, following suit. The only playable cards are the fully exposed cards at the bottom of each column. Play what cards you can to the foundations. Then build down on the topmost cards, following suit.

When there are no more moves to make, turn up the stock cards one by one, building on the foundations or the tableau and placing the unplayable cards into a wastepile. The topmost card of the wastepile is always available for play.

When all the cards of a column have been moved, fill the empty space with any of the topmost cards from the columns or the wastepile, a card from the stock, or leave it empty until you are ready to use it. There are no redeals allowed.

NAPOLEON'S SOLITAIRE

ORIGIN: French
DECK: 1 deck of 52 cards
TIME: 15 minutes
DEGREE OF DIFFICULTY: ☆

Layout

Deal the cards in two parts, as in the pages of this book. On each "page" deal four rows of five cards each and a final row of four. When the Aces show up, place them in a row at the top; these are the foundations.

How to Play

Build the Aces up to the Kings, following suit. The only playable cards are the ones at the far left and far right edges and along the bottom. The playable cards can be placed on the foundations or used to build either ascending or descending sequences on each other, always following suit. As an empty space develops, move the row on that "page" over to fill the edge space or move an entire column down to fill a space along the bottom. In this way the tableau can be shifted to bring cards into play.

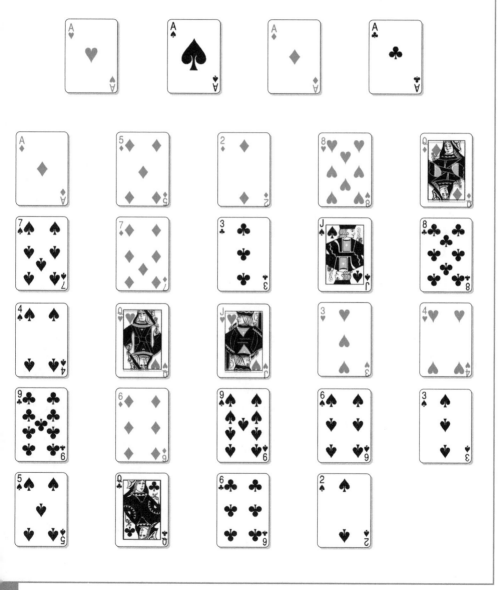

NAPOLEON'S SQUARE

☛ *(Square of Piedmont)*

ORIGIN: French
DECK: 2 decks of 52 cards
TIME: 10 minutes
DEGREE OF DIFFICULTY: ☆

Layout

Deal twelve piles of four cards each, four piles to the left (place them horizontally), four to the right (horizontally), and four across the top. Deal the cards in clockwise order, one at a time. As the Aces show up while you are dealing, place them in the center in two rows of four.

How to Play

Build on the Aces up to the Kings, following suit. Build on the piles of the tableau in descending order, always following suit. The topmost cards of the piles (and of the foundations, as described below) are available for play. Sequences of cards on the piles can also be moved to the topmost card of the other piles.

Make all the moves you can, then turn over the cards of the stock one card at a time, placing the unplayable cards in a wastepile, the topmost card of which is always available for play. If a space opens up, fill it with any available card or group of cards, or with a card from the stock or the wastepile.

It is customary with this game, bearing Napoleon's name as it does, to allow certain liberties to be taken by the player that most solitaire games do not allow. The piles can be inspected in order to study the covered cards; if you have the space, you can spread the piles slightly open to see all of the cards. Also unusual for solitaires, this game allows you to lift the cards that have been placed on the foundations and use them once again on the piles, as you see fit.

Did you know?

This Solitaire requires a lot of space since two decks of cards are used. It is said that Napoleon invented this game during his Corsican exile. The origin of the game is also claimed by the people of Piedmont, Italy, who attribute it to Victor Emanuel II instead.

NESTOR

ORIGIN: Russian
DECK: 1 deck of 52 cards
TIME: 15 minutes
DEGREE OF DIFFICULTY: ☆

Layout

Deal eight cards faceup in a row. Then deal another five rows overlapping them, so that you can see all the rows at one time. As you deal, make sure that you do not have any cards of the same rank in a column. If you are about to deal a two onto a column where a two already appears, slip the card underneath the pack and deal another card instead. You will have four cards left over; place them facedown to the side as the reserve.

How to Play

Remove the cards of the same rank by twos from the fully exposed cards at the bottom of each column. When a card from a column is removed, the next card fully exposed comes into play.

When you can't make any more moves, turn up the first card of the reserves. If that won't help you, turn up the next, and so on. Now you can see why you had to deal the rows so that two cards of the same rank were not in the same column, as that instance would inevitably block any further moves, making the game unwinnable.

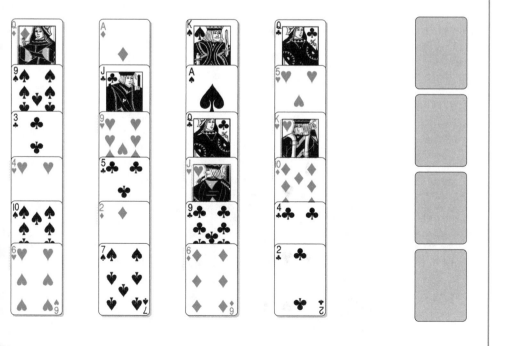

PARALLELS

ORIGIN: British
DECK: 2 decks of 52 cards
TIME: 20-25 minutes
DEGREE OF DIFFICULTY: ☆

Layout
Select a King and an Ace for each suit and place them in two columns at the sides of the tableau; these are the foundations. Between the two columns, deal a row of ten faceup cards (we show two rows of five cards below because of space constraints).

How to Play
Build down on the Kings and build up on the Aces, following suit. All cards in the rows between the foundations are playable. Spaces are not filled. When the game is blocked, deal a second row of ten cards above the first. When you deal another row of ten cards, each of these cards is playable only if there is no card directly below it. Deal another row of ten card each time the game is blocked.

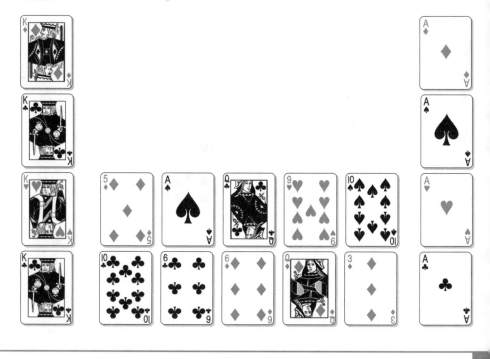

PATRIARCHS

ORIGIN: Austrian
DECK: 2 decks of 52 cards
TIME: 10 minutes
DEGREE OF DIFFICULTY: ☆ ☆ ☆

Layout

Select a King and an Ace for each suit and place them in two columns at the sides of the tableau; these are the foundations. Between the two columns, deal three rows of three cards each, which form the reserve.

How to Play

Build down on the Kings up on the Aces, following suit. When the cards on foundations of the same suit are in sequence, you can move them from one to the other, reversing the order—except Kings and Aces which do not move. All cards of the reserve are playable. Fill empty spaces with cards from the stock or with the topmost card of the wastepile. The stock is turned up one card at a time; unplayable cards are placed in the wastepile. You are allowed to redeal only once.

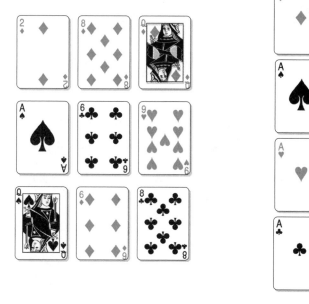

PENDULUM

☞ *(Scale)*

ORIGIN: French
DECK: 1 deck of 52 cards
TIME: 25-30 minutes
DEGREE OF DIFFICULTY: ☆ ☆ ☆

Layout

Select the four Aces and place them in a column at the right of the tableau (for reasons of space the Aces are shown at the bottom in a row on the opposite page); these are the foundations. Deal the rest of the deck in six rows of eight cards each.

How to Play

Build sequences on the foundations in ascending order, following suit; however, you decide for yourself whether to build on the Aces at intervals of one or of two. After carefully looking over the cards, you choose the best way to build: two, three, four, five, etc., up to King; or three, five, seven, etc., through Jack, King, two, four, and so on up to the Queen. This decision applies to all four foundations, as well as the playing of cards on the tableau. Only the card at the left edge of each row is playable to the foundations; the same end cards can be played on the card immediately above them in the tableau, if the card above is of the same suit and of higher rank according to the interval you have chosen.

When the game is blocked, move all of the cards from the right column to the left edge, thereby creating new possibilities of play. When the game is once again blocked, after having swung the "pendulum" to the left, you again move the right column to the left edge. The order of the remaining cards in a row will not change, except as cards are played to a row above. The "pendulum" can keep swinging as long as you still have possible moves.

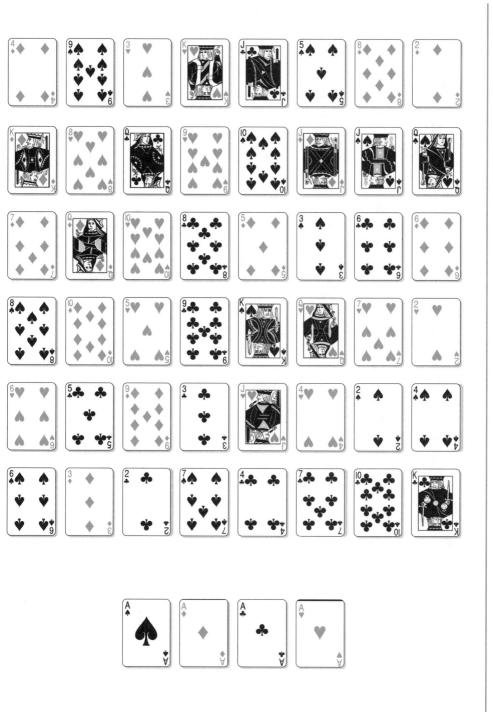

PIERRES

☞ *(Rocks)*

ORIGIN: French
DECK: 2 decks of 52 cards
TIME: 15-20 minutes
DEGREE OF DIFFICULTY: ☆

Layout

Deal two columns of six cards each. Place the top card and the bottom card of each column horizontally; these are called the pierres, or rocks. Leave enough space between the two columns for another two columns, which will be for the foundations—four Aces and four Kings, one of each suit. As you deal the first twelve cards, place an Ace or King in the middle columns, as long as one of the same suit is not already there.

How to Play

Continue dealing twelve cards at a time in the same order on the outer columns, again picking up the Kings and Aces and placing them in the middle columns, as long as one of the same suit is not already there. Build the Aces up and build the Kings down, following suit. At the beginning of the game, the first twelve cards cannot be moved on top of the foundations: only the cards that follow those can move. Also, only cards that are aligned in the same row as the foundation can be played to that foundation. However, the pierres or rocks can be played to any of the foundations.

When the cards have all been dealt, the topmost cards of the piles can be moved onto other cards of the tableau, in ascending or descending order, regardless of the suits. You can reverse the direction of building even within the same pile.

The game is successful when the each of the foundations has thirteen cards in proper sequence, following suit.

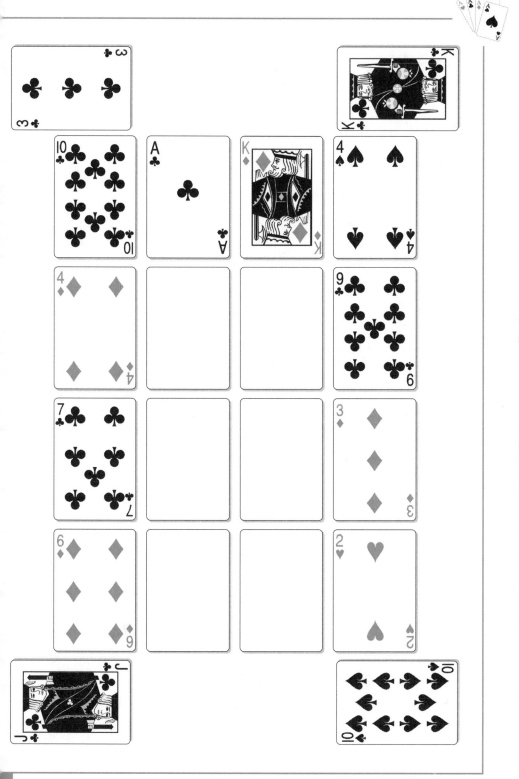

PLOT

ORIGIN: Austrian
DECK: 2 decks of 52 cards
TIME: 10 minutes
DEGREE OF DIFFICULTY: ☆

Layout

Deal a pile of thirteen cards, the topmost card of which is faceup while the rest are facedown. Place this pile at the top of the tableau; it is the reserve. Deal a fourteenth card at the upper left; whatever the rank of this card is establishes what the foundations will be for this deal. This first foundation will be the top of a column of four cards of the same rank; there will be another column of four foundation cards of the same rank at the far right. Below the reserve and between what will be the foundation columns, deal three rows of four cards each, which are the tableau. As you are dealing the tableau, as soon as they become available,

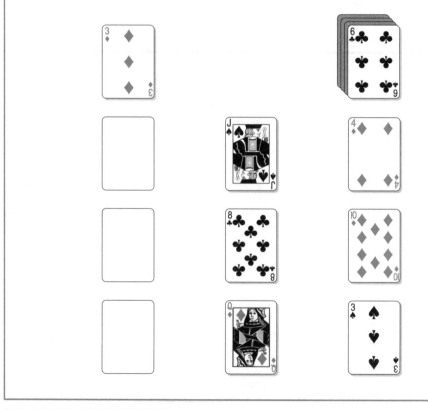

move the other seven cards of the same rank as the first foundation to their places in the two columns on either side of the tableau.

How to Play

Build up on the foundations, regardless of suit, until each foundation has thirteen cards; however, you must build the entire sequence on top of the first foundation before you can place any cards on the seven other foundations. You can build down on the cards of the tableau, regardless of suit. The topmost cards of the tableau or the reserve are playable. When a reserve card is played, turn up the card underneath.

When you have made all the moves you can with the tableau and reserve, turn the stock up one card at a time. The cards that cannot be placed on the foundations or tableau are placed in a wastepile, the topmost card of which is always available for play. Until the first foundation is complete, empty spaces can only be filled with the topmost card of the wastepile or one from the stock; however, you do not have to fill empty spaces immediately, so you can keep them open until the right card shows up. After the first foundation is complete, reserve cards can also be used to fill empty spaces. No redeal is allowed.

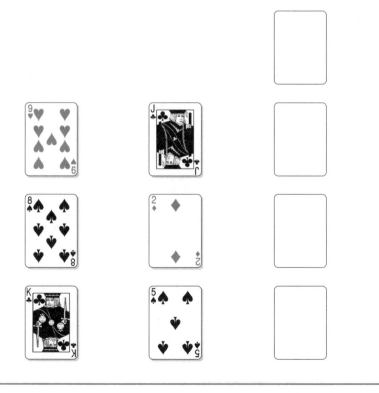

PRISONER QUEENS
☞ *(The Four Ladies)*

ORIGIN: French
DECK: 1 deck of 52 cards
TIME: 5 minutes
DEGREE OF DIFFICULTY: ☆

Layout
Select the four Queens and place them one in a pile at the center of the table. Select the four Kings and place one at the top, one underneath, and two at the sides of the Queens. Select the four Jacks and place each at an angle next to its own King. The Kings and Jacks are the foundations.

How to Play
Deal the cards of the stock one by one, using them first to build sequences, following suit, according to the patterns below:
   On the King: Ace and two;
   On the Jack: nine, seven, five, three.
   Once you have fulfilled the above sequences, the objective is to reunite each suit on the pile of its King; however, a card cannot be placed on the King pile until the card of next higher rank turns up. For example, you cannot play the three from the Jack pile to the two on the King pile of the same suit until the four turns up. Similarly, when a King pile has the sequence up to the eight, you cannot move the nine from the Jack pile of the same suit until the ten shows up.
   When spaces are freed, fill them with a card from the stock. The cards of the stock that are not playable are placed in a wastepile, the topmost card of which is always available for play. Once the stock is exhausted, you are allowed to go through wastepile twice. When each of the four Jacks is placed on the King pile of the same suit, the Prisoner Queens are released to complete the sequences.

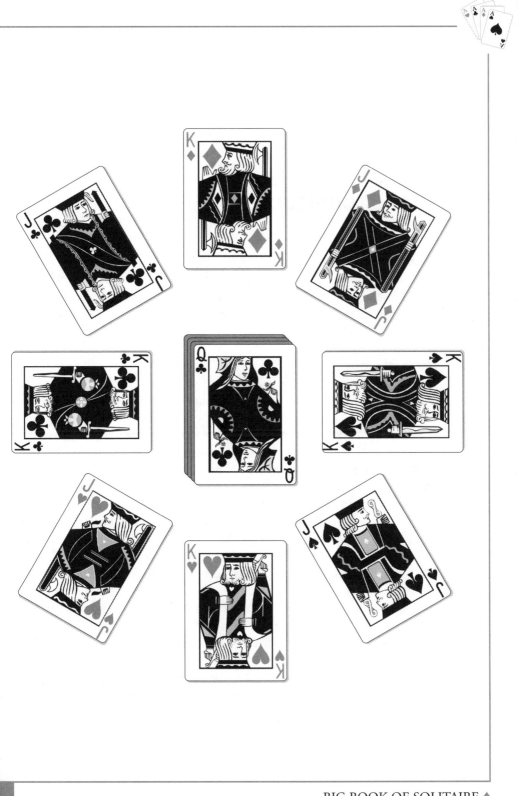

PYRAMID

☞ *(Egyptian Campaign, Pile of 28)*

ORIGIN: French
DECK: 1 deck of 52 cards
TIME: 25 minutes
DEGREE OF DIFFICULTY: ☆

Layout

Deal out the cards in the shape of a pyramid, starting with one card at the top and adding two cards that overlap it, then three overlapping them, and so on, until you have a large triangle with seven cards at the base. Each card has a numerical value equal to its rank; Kings count as 13, Queens as 12, and Jacks as 11.

How to Play

The game is played by removing pairs of cards that add up to thirteen; however, you can only remove cards that are fully exposed—not covered by another card. You can remove Kings alone, because they already count as thirteen without any help. Place all the cards you remove in a special Removed pile, faceup; the topmost card in this pile can be used again to form another match totaling thirteen.

For example, in the layout shown on the opposite page, the King can be removed alone, the ten and three can be removed as can the eight and the five; then the Queen and the Ace of the next row can be removed, and so on. When you have made all the moves you can in this way, begin turning the stock up one card at a time. Cards from the stock that are unplayable are placed faceup in a wastepile (a different pile than the Removed pile). The topmost card of the wastepile is also always available for play, and can be paired with a card from the stock, the pyramid, or the topmost card of the Removed pile. Once you have exhausted the stock, you can go through the wastepile twice.

A variation of this solitaire can be played with 40 cards. In that case, you pair the cards to total ten rather than thirteen; the stripped deck can have the eights, nines, and tens eliminated—then counting the Jacks as eight, Queens as nine, and Kings as ten—or simply remove the Jacks, Queens, and Kings instead.

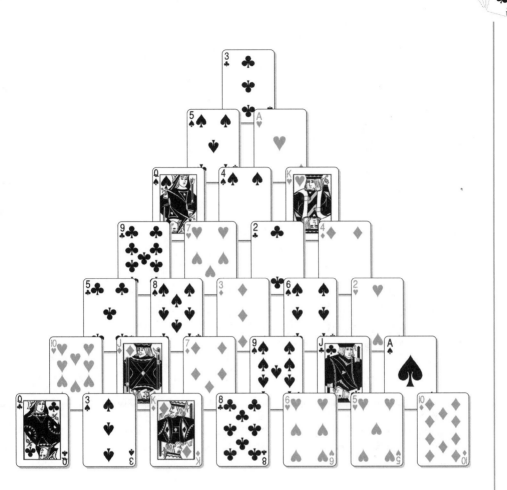

QUADRILLE

☞ *(Captive Queens, La Française, Partners)*

ORIGIN: French
DECK: 1 deck of 52 cards
TIME: 10 minutes
DEGREE OF DIFFICULTY: ☆

Layout
The layout for this game is set up as you play. The design that is to be created is shown on the opposite page.

How to Play
Start turning up the cards of the deck one at a time. As soon as the fives and sixes appear, put them in place and start building on them. On the fives you build down, following suit: four, three, two, Ace, King. On the sixes you build up, following suit: seven, eight, nine, ten, Jack. As the Queens turn up, place them in the middle; they just sit there and look regal.

The object of the game is to build the sixes up in suit to the Jacks and the fives down in suit to the Kings. You are allowed to redeal the stock twice, so that you go through the deck a total of three times.

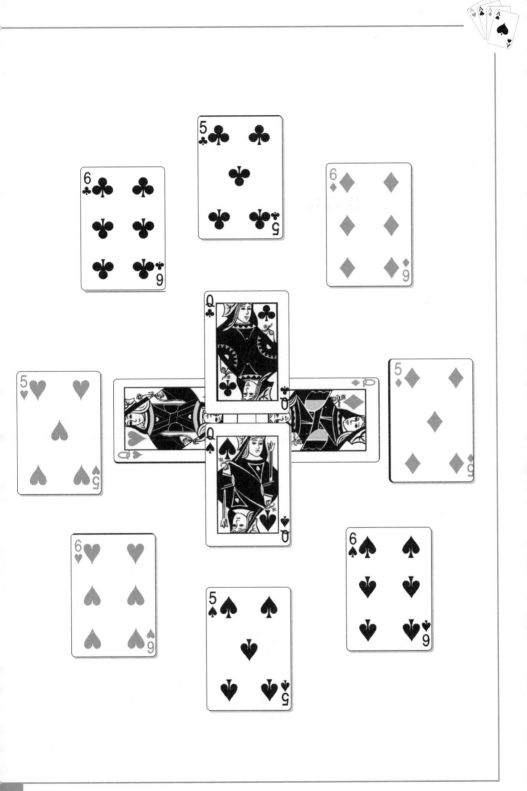

QUEEN OF ITALY

☞ *(Signora, Terrace)*

ORIGIN: Italian
DECK: 2 decks of 52 cards
TIME: 20 minutes
DEGREE OF DIFFICULTY: ☆

Layout

Deal eleven cards in a row; these are the reserve. Then deal twelve cards, choosing from these which three you want to use as the foundations. The three chosen as foundations are placed in the second row, and the other nine cards are placed in the third row beneath.

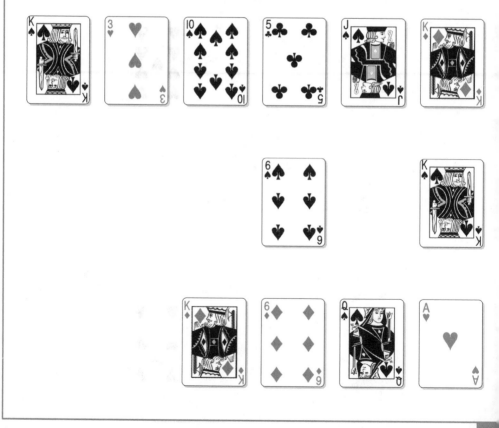

How to Play

The cards of the reserve are played one by one to the foundations; the empty spaces of the reserve are then filled with cards taken from the third row. Build on the foundations in ascending sequences of alternating colors. You can also build on top of the cards of the third row, in descending sequences of alternating colors. When you have made the moves you can, turn the stock one card at a time; the cards that cannot be played to the foundations or on the third row are placed in a wastepile, the topmost card of which is always available for play. Once you have exhausted the stock, you can go through the wastepile once.

Did you know?

This solitaire has a precise date of birth: April 21, 1868, the date of the wedding of Margaret, future Queen of Italy, with her cousin Umberto.

THE QUEEN'S NECKLACE

ORIGIN: French
DECK: 1 deck of 52 cards
TIME: 15 minutes
DEGREE OF DIFFICULTY: ☆

Layout

The layout is formed bit by bit, as the necessary cards show up. Place the four tens in the shape of a cross; These are the foundations on which you will build descending sequences, following suit from the ten down to the Ace.

How to Play

Deal the first three cards of the stock in a fan at the base of the game; when one of these three cards can be moved to its place in the layout or on the foundations, the empty space is filled with a card from the wastepile or from the stock, whatever is convenient. As you continue to deal the stock one by one, you can build ascending sequences, following suit, on the three cards of this fan. As the Queens and the Jacks show up, they are arranged in a purely ornamental necklace, as shown on the opposite page. The Kings will be placed at the center of the cross. The unplayed cards of the stock are placed in the wastepile, the topmost card of which is always available for play.

The only usable cards for forming sequences on top of the foundations—the tens—are the topmost card of the wastepile and the cards of the stock. The sequences formed on top of a card in the fan can be moved completely to their own foundation, reversing the order of the the cards as they go. Once you have exhausted the stock, you can go through the wastepile twice.

RED AND BLACK

ORIGIN: French
DECK: 2 decks of 52 cards
TIME: 15 minutes
DEGREE OF DIFFICULTY: ☆ ☆

The solitaire Red and Black is an entirely different game than the banking and gambling card games known as Red and Black, Trente et Quarante, and Rouge et Noir.

Layout

Select the eight Aces from the pack, and place them in a row at the top of the game; these are the foundations. Underneath them, deal another row of eight cards; these are the available cards.

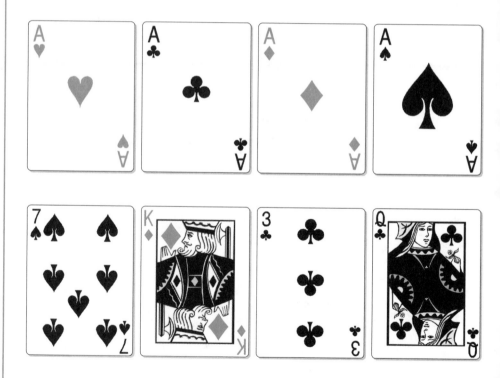

How to Play

Build on the foundations up from the Ace to the King. If, as you deal the first eight available cards, a card shows up that can be played on the Aces, it is moved to the foundation and and the empty space is filled with another card from the stock. You can build on the available cards in descending sequences in alternating colors; for example, you can place a black ten on top of a red Jack, a black Queen on top of a red King. Once you have made the initial moves, go through the stock one card at a time. Any card that cannot be played to the foundations or used to fill a space or make a sequence on the available cards is placed in a wastepile; the topmost card is always available for play. After you have exhausted the stock, you can go through the wastepile one card at a time, but only once.

It will become important as the game progresses to keep the lower ranked cards easily accessible; if they get covered in a sequence so that they are not available to play to the foundations, the game can quickly become blocked.

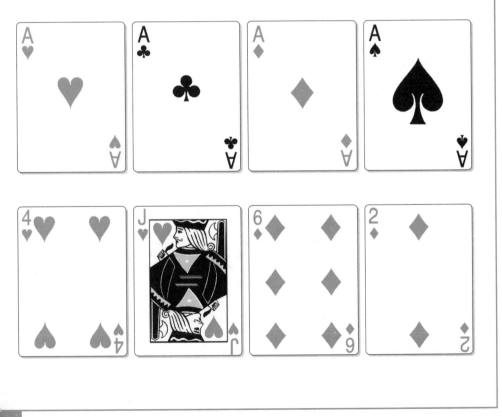

RINGS

☞ *(The Two Wedding Rings)*

ORIGIN: Italian
DECK: 2 decks of 52 cards
TIME: 20 minutes
DEGREE OF DIFFICULTY: ☆

Layout

Select all of the sixes and sevens from the pack and display them in rings of eight cards each. Place the sixes in a circle at the left and the sevens at the right; these are the foundations. Deal the first eight cards of the stock in a row underneath the rings; these are the available cards.

How to Play

Build ascending sequences on top of the sevens up to the Kings; while on top of the sixes, build descending sequences down to the Aces.

The available cards are used to build the sequences on the foundations. As you make the initial moves, if there is a space, fill it with a card from the stock; then continue by turning the stock one card at a time. Any card that cannot be played to the foundations or into an empty space in the available cards is placed into a wastepile. As you go through the stock, you can fill empty spaces from either the stock or the wastepile.

When the stock is exhausted, you can go through the wastepile once. The game is successful when you have one ring displaying all the Aces and the other ring showing all the Kings.

ROYAL APPOINTMENT

☛ *(Royal Rendezvous)*

ORIGIN: Austrian
DECK: 2 decks of 52 cards
TIME: 20 minutes
DEGREE OF DIFFICULTY: ☆

Layout

Select all of the Aces and lay them out in two rows, with an Ace of each suit in each row. Select a two of each suit and place two to the left of the second row of Aces and two to the right; the eight Aces and four twos are the foundations. Beneath the row of twos and Aces, deal two rows of eight cards faceup; these are the reserve.

How to Play

Build on the foundations: On top of the top row of Aces, build up to Queens, following suit; on the bottom row of Aces, build up by twos to Kings to have Ace, three, five, seven, nine, Jack, King; on the twos, build up by twos to Queens to have two, four, six, eight, ten, Queen; the second four Kings are placed to cap the top foundations only if their matching King has already been placed in its sequence on the second row of Aces.

All the reserve cards can be played on the foundations. Go through the stock, one card at a time, building on the foundations or discarding into a wastepile, the topmost card of which is always available for play. Fill an empty space in the bottom two rows with the topmost card of the wastepile, or, if there isn't any, with a card from the stock. You are only allowed to deal once.

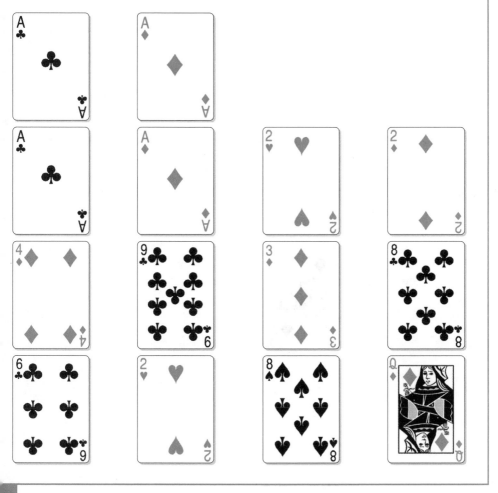

ROYAL AUDIENCE

ORIGIN: French
DECK: 1 deck of 52 cards
TIME: 20 minutes
DEGREE OF DIFFICULTY: ☆

Layout

Deal sixteen cards faceup with four to the left, four at the top, four at the right, and four at the bottom. Spread these cards out enough to allow twelve cards to be placed in the center as shown in the layout on the opposite page. The outer sixteen cards are called the antechamber, and the inner twelve cards will be the audience hall.

How to Play

If among the first sixteen cards there are any Kings, Queens, or Aces, these are placed at the center of the game; the King of Spades at the center top with the Queen of Spades underneath; the King of Clubs at the center bottom with the Queen of Clubs above; the King of Hearts at the far right with the Queen of Hearts to the inside; and the King of Diamonds at the far left with the Queen of Diamonds to the inside; each Ace is placed diagonally just to the side of its respective Queen. The Kings and Queens are decorative; the Aces are the foundations. Build on the Aces up to the Jacks, following suit.

Go through the stock one card at a time, filling a space in the antechamber, adding a King, Queen, or Ace to the audience hall as they show up, building on the foundations, or adding to a wastepile, the topmost card of which is always available for play. The game is successful when there are no more "people" waiting in the antechamber; all have been given a royal audience. The topmost card of the foundations reveals the official who has made the introductions.

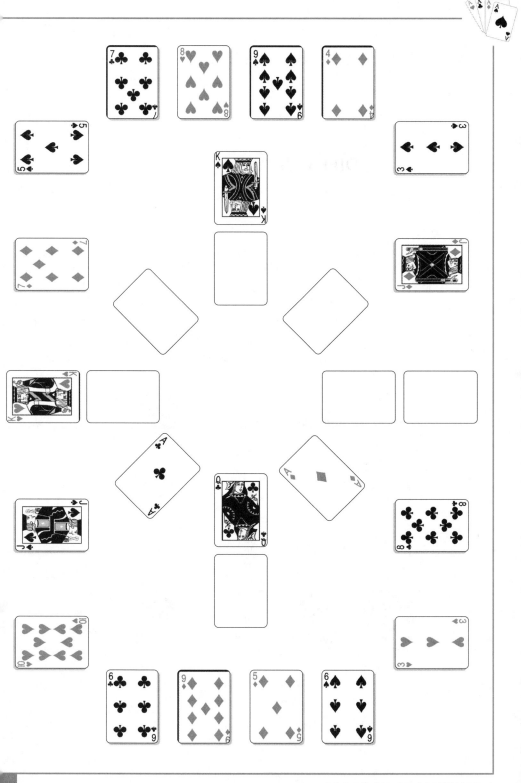

ROYAL COTILLION

☞ *(Contredanse)*

ORIGIN: Italian
DECK: 2 decks of 52 cards
TIME: 15 minutes
DEGREE OF DIFFICULTY: ☆ ☆

Layout

Select an Ace and a two of each suit, and set out the Aces in one column and the twos in another column to the right of the Aces; these are the foundations. To the left of the Ace column, deal twelve cards faceup in three rows of four cards each. To the right of the two column, deal sixteen cards faceup in four rows of four cards each. (Some players prefer to establish the foundations by placing the Aces and twos as they come into play; but keep in mind that you need one of each suit.)

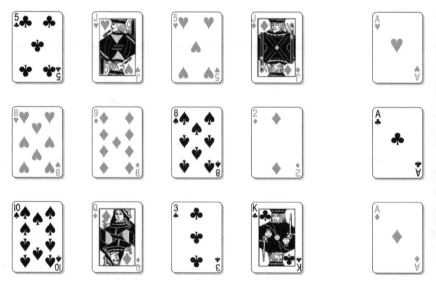

How to Play

Build up the foundations by twos, following suit, in these patterns: on the Aces, three, five, seven, nine, Jack, King, two, four, six, eight, ten, Queen; on the twos, four, six, eight, ten, Queen, Ace, three, five, seven, nine, Jack, King. Any of the cards in the right four columns are available for play; space in the right four columns must be filled immediately from the wastepile or from the stock if there is no wastepile. Only the bottom cards of the four columns on the left are available for play to the foundations; spaces in the left three rows are not filled. Cards in the second and top rows on the left cannot be played until the ones immediately below have been moved away.

After making what moves you can from the left and right columns to the foundations, turn the stock, one card at a time, playing it to the foundations, filling a space in the right four columns, or placing it into a wastepile, the topmost card of which is always available for play. You can only go through the cards once; there is no redeal.

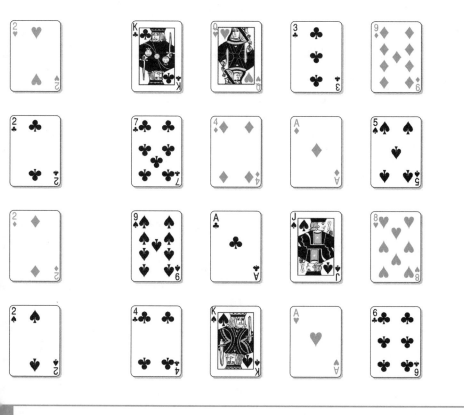

ROYAL COURT

ORIGIN: French
DECK: 1 deck of 52 cards
TIME: 15 minutes
DEGREE OF DIFFICULTY: ☆

Layout

Deal the cards in the shape of a rectangle with right and left sides of five cards, called East and West, and top and bottom sides of four cards, called North and South. Arrange the four Kings, as they show up, in a row at the center of the court; these are the foundations.

How to Play

Build on the foundations from King down to Ace, following suit. The East and West cards can only be played to the foundations, and are not otherwise moved. The North and South cards can not only be played to the foundations, but can also be moved to build ascending sequences in the same color on other cards of the North and South sides.

Go through the stock one card at a time, filling spaces in the sides, playing to sequences on the North or South sides, or discarding in a wastepile, the topmost card of which is always available for play. You are not required to move a card to the foundations if keeping it in its place is more convenient for bringing the game to a successful conclusion. Once the stock is exhausted, you are allowed to go through the wastepile once.

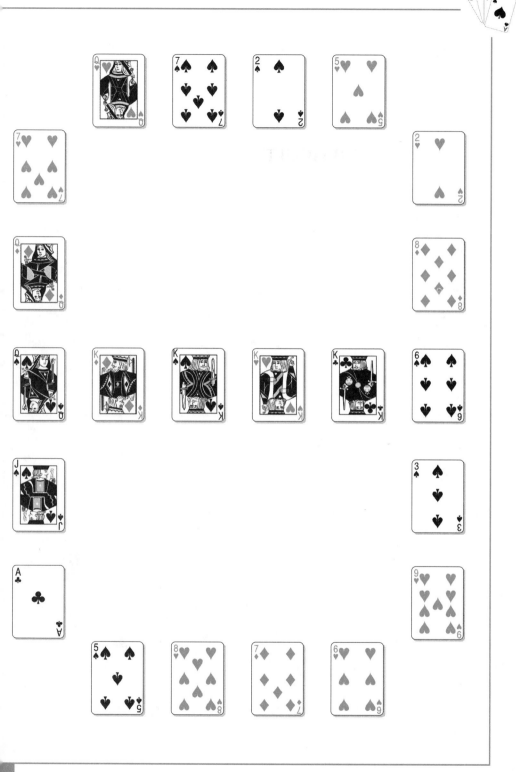

ROYAL PALACE

ORIGIN: French
DECK: 2 decks of 52 cards
TIME: 15 minutes
DEGREE OF DIFFICULTY: ☆

Layout
Deal four rows of eight cards each on the tableau. Place an Ace and a King of each suit in two columns, at either side of the rows, as they show up; these are the foundations.

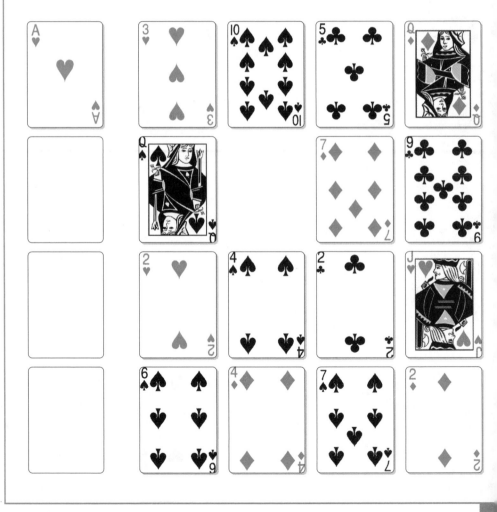

How to Play

Build up on the Aces and build down on the Kings, following suit. The cards of the tableau are playable only if they are free, meaning that there is no card below them in the tableau; playable cards are at the bottom of a column or have an empty space below them. Empty spaces, created either by placing Aces and Kings to start foundation piles or by playing other cards to the foundation piles, should not be filled.

When the game is blocked, collect the cards displayed in the rows of the tableau and, without shuffling, deal them again into rows of eight, in reverse order to the last deal. Fill out the full four rows of eight with cards from the stock. You are allowed to go through the stock only once.

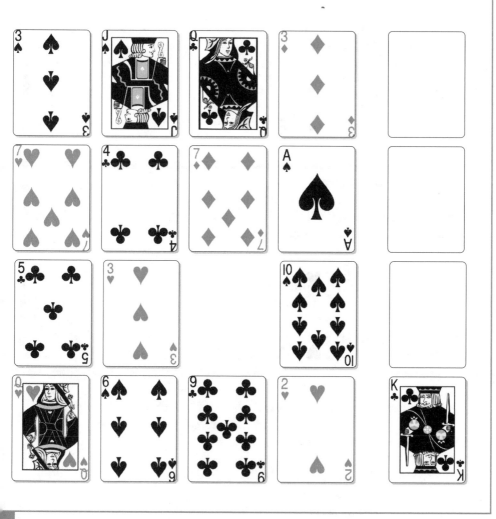

BIG BOOK OF SOLITAIRE ♦

RUSSIAN BANK

☞ *(Crapette)*

ORIGIN: Russia
DECK: 2 decks of 52 cards (one for each player)
TIME: 45 minutes
DEGREE OF DIFFICULTY: ☆ ☆ ☆

Layout

Each player has a deck of 52 cards with a distinctive back. The players draw one card each from one of the decks; the lower card has the right to play first, alternating turns thereafter. The King is high and the Ace is low. The players shuffle and cut their opponent's deck. Each player deals to their right a pile of twelve cards facedown, as a reserve, then deals a column of four cards faceup above the reserve; these columns are the tableau. As the Aces come into play, they will be laid out in two columns in the center; the Aces are the foundations.

How to Play

The objective is for each player to play his or her entire deck onto the foundations, the tableau, or the opponent's reserve or wastepile. Build the foundations up from Ace to King, following suit. Build down on the tableau in alternating colors, overlapping cards to the side so that all cards are visible. Building on the foundations always takes precedence. An empty space in the tableau can be filled from the top card of another tableau pile, the player's reserve, or, when that is exhausted, from the player's stock; spaces do not have to be filled as soon as they occur.

The opening turns of the game must be started by moving any available card from the tableau to the center, then turning up the top card of that player's reserve, and playing that card to the center; if the reserve card cannot be played to the center, it may be played elsewhere on the tableau. If the reserve card is still not playable, the player can then draw a card from his or her stock. It is still the players turn until the card from the stock cannot be played; then it is placed faceup into a wastepile at the player's left. In subsequent turns, players can turn over the top card of their reserve prior to making a play, and are not obligated to play it.

The playable cards are the topmost cards of the tableau, of the reserve, or of the stock. If a player can build to the center with a choice of cards, the reserve card must be used before cards from the tableau or stock. Card of the wastepile cannot be played until all of the player's stock is exhausted; then they are turned as a unit facedown.

Once all available cards have been played to the center, the player has the option of "loading" cards onto the opponent's reserve or wastepile in up or down sequences, following suit. If the opponent's reserve card is facedown, the player can ask at any time for it to be turned faceup.

If a player thinks his opponent has broken the rules, he may call "Stop," and play must be halted. If the mistake is proven, the wrongly played card returned to its original place and the turn ends.

The winner scores 30 points, plus two points for each card of the opponent's reserve and one point for each of the opponent's stock and wastepile. In case of a draw, players can evaluate their remaining cards.

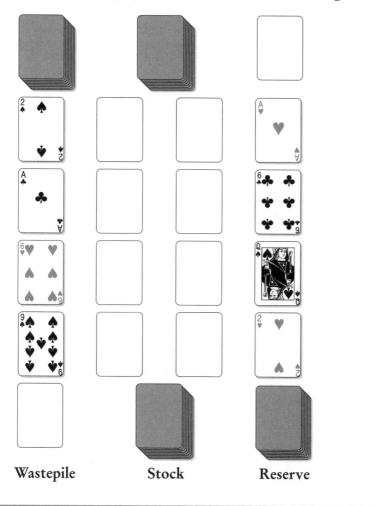

Wastepile   Stock   Reserve

SALIC LAW

ORIGIN: British
DECK: 2 decks of 52 cards
TIME: 15 minutes
DEGREE OF DIFFICULTY: ☆

Layout
Remove the eight Queens, which don't enter into the game, and set them aside. Select a King of any suit, and place it at the upper left of the tableau; the layout is constructed as the game proceeds. The Aces are the foundations, and will be placed, as they turn up, in a row at the very top.

How to Play
The objective is to build on the Aces up to the Jacks, regardless of suit. The game proceeds as you begin dealing on top of the King you placed at the upper left. Deal the cards faceup in a downward-overlapping fan; when another King shows up, place it to the right of the first King and start dealing the cards below it as before. As the Aces show up, place them in the foundation row above the Kings. Even while you are still dealing, you can build on the foundations, using the topmost cards of the downward fans.

Keep dealing the cards until all of the cards have been dealt; at that point all eight of the Kings will have been placed at the top of a downward fan. Once all cards have been dealt, and a downward fan on a King has been removed, you can place the King on any foundation that is built up to the Jack, and fill the empty space in the tableau with any of the topmost cards.

Did you know?

This game refers to an ancient rule said to derive from the legal code of the Salic Franks that excluded females from the line of succession to a throne. This law had special notoriety during the fight for succession to the crown between Edward III of England and Philip IV of Wales.

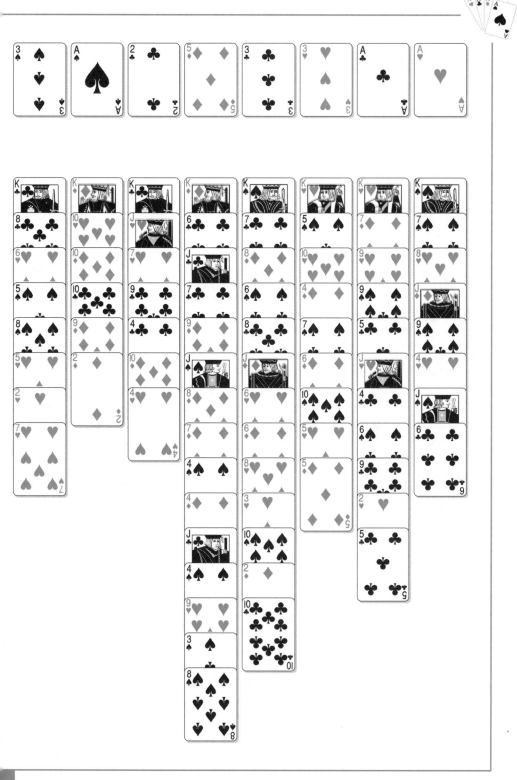

SCORPION

☞ *(Castle of Antwerp, Lieges)*

ORIGIN: Belgian
DECK: 1 deck of 52 cards
TIME: 10 minutes
DEGREE OF DIFFICULTY: ☆ ☆

Layout

Deal a row of seven cards with the first four facedown and the last three faceup. Deal a second and a third row in the same way, overlapping the cards from the previous row. Then deal four more rows of seven cards each, all faceup, overlapping as before. You will have three cards left over at the end; place these below the rows as a reserve.

How to Play

The aim of the game is to reduce, with appropriate building, the number of the columns from seven to four: a column for each suit. The four Kings become the foundations on which you build down to the Aces, following suit. But the Kings are not removed from the tableau.

Proceed by building down on the exposed cards, following suit. You are not limited to moving one card at a time, you may move any card that is of the right rank and suit—even if it is covered with cards. All the cards on top of the card you want to move are moved with it. Nothing can be built on an Ace.

When a column is emptied, the space does not need to be filled immediately, but it can be filled with a King—along with all of the cards that are on top of it.

When you have exhausted all the moves you can make, not including a space that you may later fill, take the three cards that you have as reserve and place one on each of the bottom cards of the left-hand columns.

As each facedown card is reached—by removal of the cards on top— the card is turned faceup. The "sting" of the *Scorpion* game is that an unwary player may be caught at the tail end of the game if the hidden cards have not been uncovered soon enough.

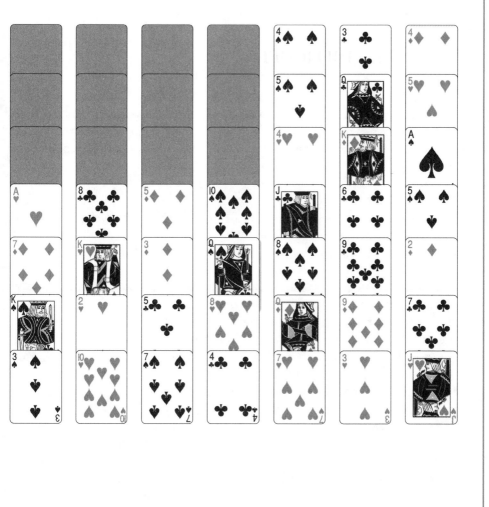

SLY FOX

☞ *(Twenty)*

ORIGIN: Russian
DECK: 2 decks of 52 cards
TIME: 20 minutes
DEGREE OF DIFFICULTY: ☆ ☆

Layout

Place four Aces, one of each suit, in a column on the left; place four Kings, one of each suit, in a column on the right. Deal twenty cards in between the Aces and Kings—either five rows of four cards each, or four rows of five cards each.

How to Play

Build the Aces up to the Kings and build the Kings down to the Aces, following suit. Build on the foundations using the cards in the middle of the layout. As each space opens up, immediately fill it with a card from the stock.

When the game is blocked, start going through the stock, one card at a time. You cannot play from the middle cards for the moment. Play a card from the stock to a foundation, if you can; if you cannot, then place the card on one of the twenty cards in the middle—the choice of where is yours. As you place it, count it, but don't count the ones you are able to place on the foundations. You must continue playing cards from the stock until you have counted twenty cards that you have placed on the middle cards. When you reach twenty, stop going through the stock. Now you can make new plays from the middle cards that have become possible, but this time do not fill spaces from the stock.

Each time the game becomes blocked, you must start going through the stock again, and as before, after you place twenty cards in the middle, stop going through the stock and make the moves you can to the foundations.

Pay attention to your plan for placing cards and you may be the Sly Fox. Scattering cards may be necessary to avoid being blocked; having one pile for Aces and Kings, paired by suit, may help, since they will be wanted last.

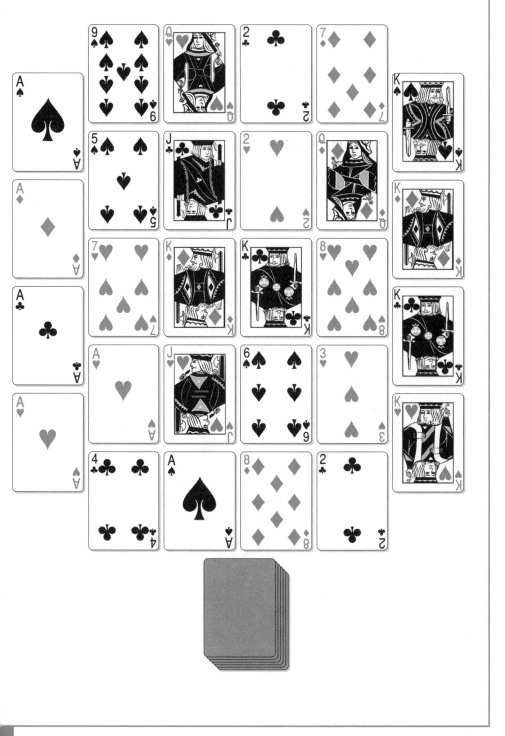

SPIDER

ORIGIN: Russian
DECK: 2 decks of 52 cards
TIME: 20 minutes
DEGREE OF DIFFICULTY: ☆ ☆ ☆ ☆

Layout
Deal out 54 cards in ten piles as follows: six cards in the first four piles, five cards in the last six piles. Only the topmost cards should be faceup. These files are the foundations and the tableau at the same time, and all action takes place on them.

To Win the Game
Build eight sequences in downward order from Kings to Aces right on the tableau. Once a sequence is built, it is discarded. So to win the game is to clear the entire tableau of cards.

How to Play

After you deal out the cards, make all the moves that you can, building down, regardless of suit. Note, however, that even though you are *permitted* to build regardless of suit, you will limit yourself when you do it. You are permitted to move a group of cards as a unit only when they are in the same suit and in correct rank—so while you would never be able to win the game making only moves that were in suit, it is certainly better to build in suit, if you have the choice.

When you move an entire pile, leaving an empty space, you may move any available card or group of cards into it. Keep in mind that a King cannot move, except into an empty space. It cannot be placed on an Ace.

When you cannot make any more moves, deal ten more cards, one on each pile. All spaces must be filled before you are allowed to deal another ten cards onto the layout. And again, make whatever moves you can. Follow this procedure for the entire game, dealing another ten cards whenever you're blocked.

After you have put together a complete sequence, you do not have to discard it right away. You may be able to use its cards to help build other sequences.

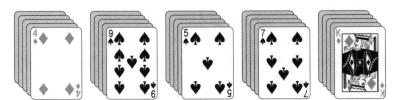

STAIRCASE

☞ *(Imperial Stairs, Royal Staircase)*

ORIGIN: Russian
DECK: 1 deck of 52 cards
TIME: 5 minutes
DEGREE OF DIFFICULTY: ☆ ☆

Layout

Deal a row of five cards facedown, and then deal the rest of the deck onto the five piles, one row at a time. The first two piles will have one card more than the others. This is a game of chance.

How to Play

The object is to go from five piles to four, to three, and so on—like a staircase—until you have isolated the five cards of a royal flush. Start by turning the topmost card of the first pile faceup; if you find an Ace (high), a court card, or a ten—the rank of the cards that in Poker make a royal flush—then this card establishes the suit of the royal flush for this game. If you don't find one of these cards, set it aside, and keep turning up the cards on the first pile until you come to one. Once you have the first royal flush card, move onto the next pile and turn up the cards, setting them aside until you come to another of the cards of the royal flush. Go through the next pile in the same way. If there is no card of the royal flush in a pile, the entire pile is set aside. Then turn over the face up cards and pick up the piles, and deal out the cards again, this time into four piles. Repeat the same operation with three piles, and so on, until you have only one pile. If the game is successful, this pile will be the five cards of the royal straight flush.

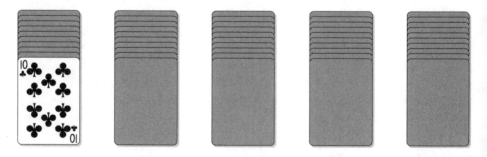

THIRTEEN

ORIGIN: French
DECK: 1 deck of 52 cards
TIME: 10 minutes
DEGREE OF DIFFICULTY: ☆

Layout

Deal a row of five cards, faceup. Then deal two cards, facedown, in a row below them; these are the reserve. The remaining cards of the deck are the stock.

How to Play

The object of the game is to get rid of all the cards, by eliminating, in pairs, cards whose rank adds up to thirteen. You need to keep in mind that the Queen's rank is twelve, the Jack's is eleven, and the Ace's is one. The pairs that add up to thirteen are removed from the table and laid aside. Kings are eliminated by themselves, as they show up or before dealing the cards. Deal another row of five cards on top of the first one, and again remove cards that add up to thirteen. You can use only the topmost card of each pile for pairing. If, after dealing five new cards, there is no pair, turn over one of the reserve cards before redealing. Fill a space in the reserve with a facedown card from the stock. If you are successful at removing all of the cards, you've won the game.

Some players prefer to wait until they've gone through the entire pack before turning over the two leftover cards of the reserve.

THIRTEEN WISE MEN

☞ *(Thirteen Piles, Game of Thirteen)*

ORIGIN: French
DECK: 1 deck of 52 cards
TIME: 5 minutes
DEGREE OF DIFFICULTY: ☆

Layout

Deal thirteen piles of four cards each in two rows; one row of seven piles the second row of six. The cards should be facedown, except for the topmost card which will be turned faceup after all piles have been dealt. As the Aces show up, place them in a third row below the tableau; these are the foundations.

How to Play

Build on the foundations from Ace up to King, following suit. You can build down on the topmost cards of the thirteen piles, regardless of suit. The topmost card of each pile is playable, as is the card underneath after the one on top has been removed. If when turning a card you find a King, place it underneath the pile you have found it in.

When one of the thirteen piles is exhausted, the empty space can not be filled under any circumstances. Thus, it is better, before moving the last card of a pile, to consider whether waiting may allow more chances to release other cards for play.

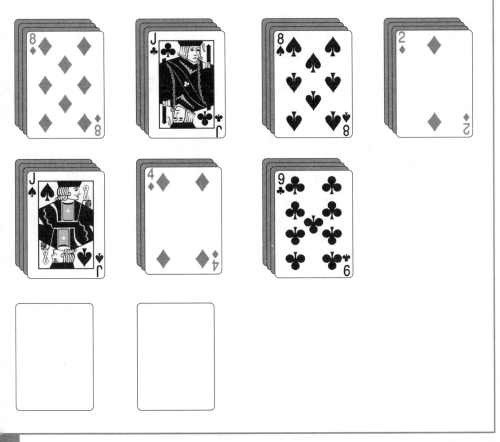

BIG BOOK OF SOLITAIRE ♦

THRILLER

☞ *(Captain Scary, Suspense)*

ORIGIN: Italian
DECK: 1 deck of 52 cards
TIME: 10 minutes
DEGREE OF DIFFICULTY: ☆ ☆

Layout

Deal five piles of four cards each with the topmost card faceup, except for the central pile; the pile with the card facedown is called the center, while the piles at its sides are called wings.

How to Play

The object of the game is to build all of the cards on the foundations, which are revealed as the game proceeds. Turn the cards of the stock over one by one, playing them to the wings or into a wastepile. Play the faceup cards from the wings to the wastepile, as you are able. You can

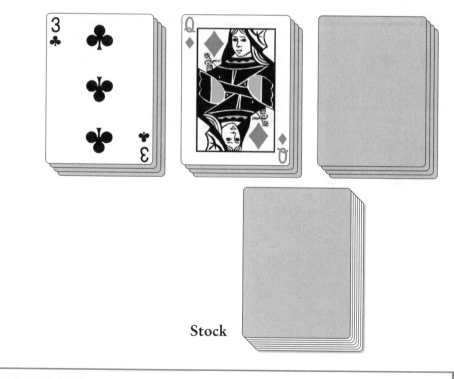

Stock

build descending or ascending sequences on the wings and the wastepile, regardless of suit, changing order as you wish; for example, two, three, four, three, two.

When you succeed in eliminating the faceup cards of the wings by moving them from the tableau and placing them in the wastepile, you turn the first card of the center faceup and place it at the right of the game; this card establishes the first foundation on which to build sequences. Then you turn up the next cards on the wings, and proceed as before.

Once you have four cards placed as the foundations, the solitaire proceeds in a different way: instead of taking the cards of the wings to the wastepile, you need to build sequences only on the foundations, always in ascending or descending order, regardless of suit, and changing the order as you wish.

When the game is blocked, deal another four cards faceup on the wings; you can go through the wastepile once in the same manner. The sooner you can uncover the facedown cards, the more likely you may be able to have a successful game.

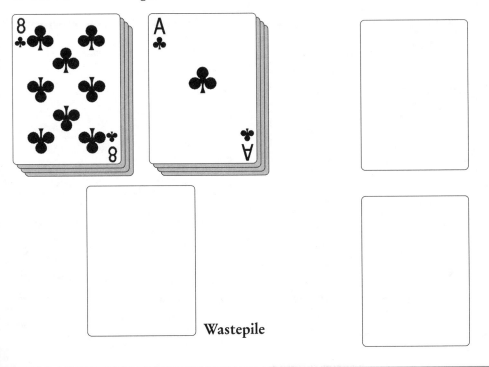

Wastepile

BIG BOOK OF SOLITAIRE ♦

TOURNAMENT

☛ *(Kibitzer and Dormitzer, Paladins and Saracens)*

ORIGIN: French
DECK: 2 decks of 52 cards
TIME: 15 minutes
DEGREE OF DIFFICULTY: ☆ ☆

Layout

Deal at the sides of the game, to the right and the left, two columns of four cards each which are the reserve and are called kibitzers. If no Aces or Kings appear among them, put the cards back, shuffle, and deal again. Between the two columns of the kibitzers, deal six fanned piles of four cards each that overlap downward; these are called the dormitzers. As the Aces and Kings become available, place one of each suit at the top of the tableau.

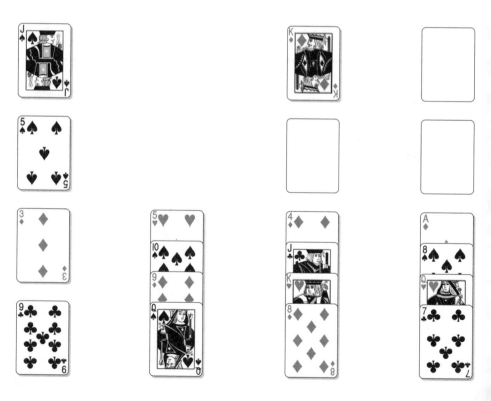

How to Play

Build the Aces up to the Kings and build the Kings down to the Aces, following suit. All the kibitzers as well as the fully exposed cards of the dormitzers are available for play to the foundations. An empty space in the kibitzers can be filled with any fully exposed card of the dormitzers, at your convenience; however, an empty space in the dormitzers, meaning a whole column has been removed, must be filled immediately with four new cards dealt from the stock.

Make whatever moves you can from the dormitzers and the kibitzers to the foundations. When the game is blocked, deal four new cards to each of the six piles of the dormitzers; if there are less than twenty-four cards, just put them down as far as they will go.

Sequences on the foundations may be moved from one to the other when the cards on top are of the same suit and in sequence.

You are allowed to redeal the dormitzers twice, but in each case pick up the last pile of the dormitzers first so that the order of the deal is changed.

TREASURE ISLAND

☞ *(Found Treasure, Osmosis, Peek)*

ORIGIN: Belgian
DECK: 1 deck of 52 cards
TIME: 5 minutes
DEGREE OF DIFFICULTY: ☆ ☆ ☆

Layout

Deal four piles of four cards each, facedown, and arrange them in a column at the left side of the playing space. Then deal the next card faceup and place it to the right of the top pile; this card is the first foundation and establishes the rank of the other three foundations, which are placed as they become available in the play of the game.

How to Play

Build on the foundations following suit, but without regard to the sequence of rank; overlap the foundation cards to the right so that they are all visible. You can place any card of the same suit on top of the first foundation card; however, no card may be placed on the second foundation until the card of the same rank has already been placed on the first foundation. Similarly, no card may be placed on the third foundation until the card of the same rank has already been placed on the second foundation row; and no card can be placed on the fourth foundation until the same rank has been played on the third.

Go through the cards of the stock, three at a time, to find playable cards, placing the unplayed cards in a wastepile, the topmost card of which is still available for play. Some players prefer to go through the cards one at a time; either way there is no limit to the number of times you can go through the cards. The game ends when the foundation piles each have thirteen cards of the same suit or when the game is blocked.

The variation of this game known as Peek is played exactly the same way, except the facedown cards are turned up so that each can be seen.

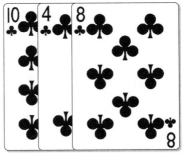

TWO CONSULS

ORIGIN: French
DECK: 2 decks of 52 cards
TIME: 10 minutes
DEGREE OF DIFFICULTY: ☆

Layout

Select the eight twos and place them in two rows at the center; these are the foundations. Around the three sides of the foundations, deal ten cards, four directly above the twos and three at each side; these are the tableau.

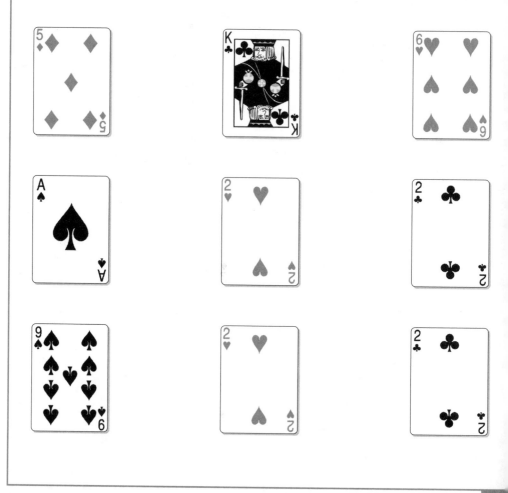

How to Play

Build the foundations—the twos—up to the Aces, which will be placed after the Kings, following suit. You can build down on the tableau—the ten cards placed on the sides—also always following suit. You can move more than one card from one place in the tableau to another if they create a sequence in the new location. The topmost cards of the tableau are playable.

Turn the cards of the stock one at a time and play them to the foundations or to the tableau. Unplayable cards are placed in a wastepile, the topmost card of which is always available for play. Fill empty spaces in the tableau with cards from the stock or the wastepile, but not other cards from the tableau. You only get to go through the stock once; you cannot go through the wastepile.

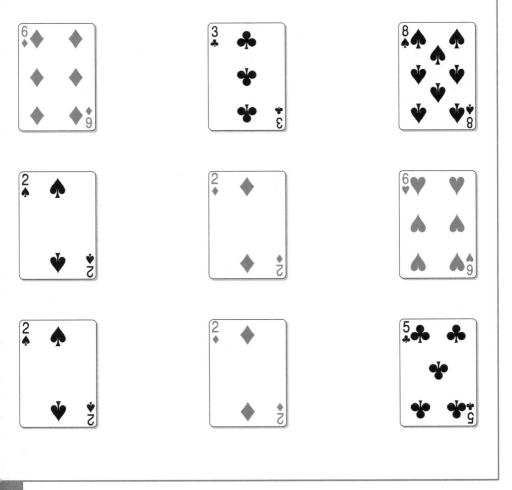

VIENNESE WEAVERS

☛ *(Leoni's Own, Weavers)*

ORIGIN: Austrian
DECK: 2 decks of 52 cards
TIME: 20 minutes
DEGREE OF DIFFICULTY: ☆ ☆ ☆ ☆

Layout

Select from the pack an Ace and a King of each suit and place them in two rows with the Kings at the top; these are the foundations. Below them, deal two rows of faceup cards and a thirteenth card at the bottom right at a slight angle. As you deal them out, count to yourself, "Ace, two, three, four, five, six, seven, eight, nine, ten, Jack, Queen, King," as labeled in the layout on the opposite page. If, as you are dealing, the card you name appears as you name it, that card is an "Exile," and is placed at the top left, facedown. Deal another card in its place. Continue in this way, dealing out the entire stock; the "King" pile at the lower right is spread out so you can see all of its cards.

How to Play

When all the cards have been laid out, you can begin building what you can to the foundations, building the Kings down and the Aces up, following suit. When the game is blocked, turn over the top card of the Exiles pile. If the Exile card can be played to a foundation, you must play it. If it cannot, place it at the bottom of the pile that corresponds to its rank; for example, a four is slipped underneath the fourth pile. Then take the topmost card of that pile and slip it underneath its pile until you have uncovered a card that you can play; for example, after the four is slipped under the fourth pile, if the top card is a two, then it goes under the two pile, and so forth. If you turn up a King, it is placed under the King pile, but play stops; you then turn up another Exile card.

When the Ace and the King foundations of the same suit are in sequence, you can move all the cards from one to the other, except the original Ace or King. You are allowed to redeal the cards twice, collecting the piles in reverse order so the King pile is on top and the Ace pile is next to the bottom, with the bottom being the Exile cards.

Exiles

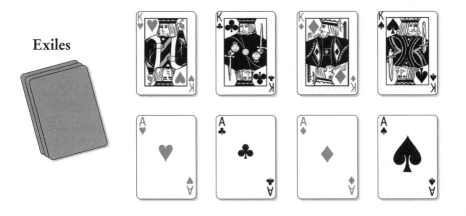

Ace	Two	Three	Four	Five	Six

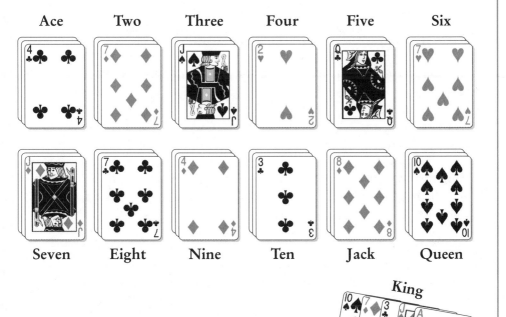

Seven	Eight	Nine	Ten	Jack	Queen

King

VIRGINIA REEL

☞ *(Blue Jacket)*

ORIGIN: American
DECK: 2 decks of 52 cards
TIME: 30 minutes
DEGREE OF DIFFICULTY: ☆ ☆ ☆

Layout

Select a two, three, and four of different suits and place them in a column at the left; these are the first three of twelve foundations—the other foundations will be the the cards of the same rank when they are moved into the row beside one of the foundations. To the right of the first foundations, deal seven faceup cards. Below these three rows, deal a row of eight cards; these are the reserve.

How to Play

Build the foundations up, following suit, according to these patterns: two, five, eight, Jack; three, six, nine, Queen; four, seven, ten, King.

The reserve cards can be played on the foundations; the cards of the rows, other than the foundation cards, can also be played to the foundations, but only if the empty space is filled immediately by a two, three, or four, according to the row into which the card is placed. As the twos, threes, and fours are moved to the corresponding row, they become foundations themselves. The Aces are unusable and are removed from the game, but are always substituted for by a two, three, or four, as appropriate, if they come from one of the rows that has a foundation card.

When the game is blocked, deal another eight cards on top of those of the reserve. Only the topmost cards of the reserve can be played on the foundations or, if it is a two, three or four, it can be used to replace cards that are played from the rows containing the foundations. The empty spaces in the reserve are not filled other than by next deal of eight cards. The Aces in the reserve are removed, without substitution. You are not allowed to redeal.

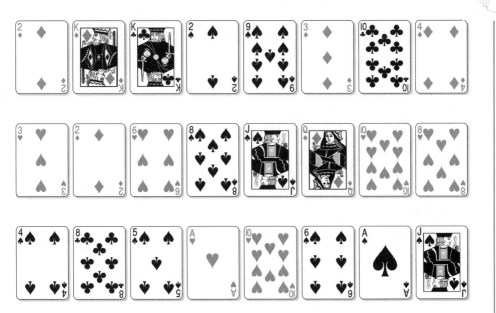

Did you know?

This game became fashionable during the American Civil War. The reel is a dance.

WINDMILL

☞ *(Propeller)*

ORIGIN: Belgian
DECK: 2 decks of 52 cards
TIME: 5 minutes
DEGREE OF DIFFICULTY: ☆ ☆

Layout
Select any Ace and place it at the center of the game; this is one of five foundations. Then deal two cards in each direction to form the "blades" or "sails" of the windmill.

How to Play
Go through the stock, one card at a time. As Kings become available, place one of them to each side of the windmill blades, as shown in the layout on the opposite page; these are the other four foundations.

Build up on the Ace regardless of suit, placing another Ace on top after you reach the King, until there are fifty-two cards—four times through the Ace to King sequence. Build down on the Kings, also regardless of suit, so that each King has thirteen cards in sequence from King to Ace.

You can use the cards that are in the windmill blades for building on the foundations, as well as the topmost card of the stock or wastepile. The unplayable cards of the stock are placed in the wastepile. When a space opens up in the blades of the windmill, fill it when you want to with the topmost card of the wastepile or, if there are no cards in the wastepile, fill it from the stock.

You are allowed to move the topmost card from a King foundation to play on the Ace foundation, but only one at a time; that is, the next card to go on the Ace foundation must come from the windmill blades, the stock, or the wastepile.

Some players prefer the central foundation card to be a King and the other four foundations to be Aces. With this alternative, four descending sequences are built on top of the King and ascending sequences are built on each of the four Aces. In either version, the stock is only gone through once.

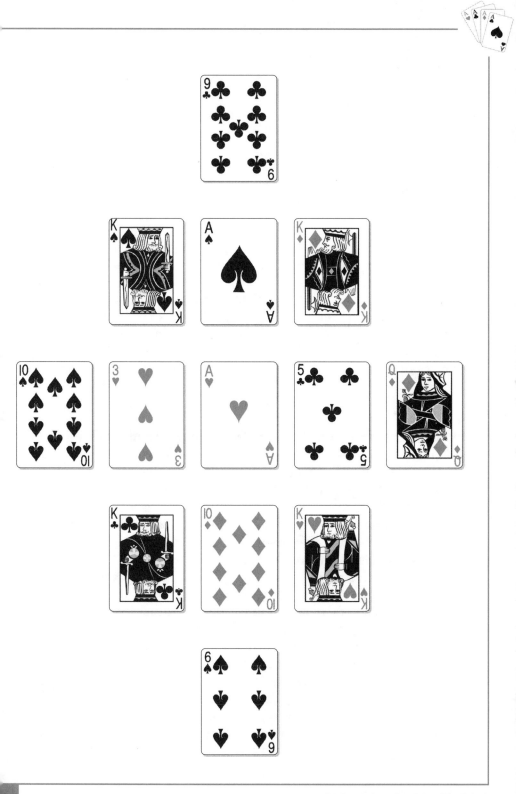

YUKON

☞ *(Russian Solitaire)*

ORIGIN: Russian
DECK: 1 deck of 52 cards
TIME: 20 minutes
DEGREE OF DIFFICULTY: ☆ ☆ ☆

Layout

Deal seven cards in a row—facedown except for the first card. Then put the eighth card faceup on the second card in the row and complete a new row with facedown cards. Place a faceup card on the third pile, and finish off the row in the same way. Continue, just as for Klondike, until you have a faceup card on every pile. Deal the remaining 24 cards faceup on the six columns to the right of the first card, as shown in the layout on the opposite page. Aces that are faceup at the bottom of a column are placed in a row at the top of the game; these are the foundations.

How to Play

Build on the Aces up to Kings, following suit. The bottom card of each column can be built down in alternating colors; for example, a black three can be added to a red four. But unlike Klondike, you can move any card that is faceup, not just the bottom card. Even if a card is buried in the middle of a column, it can be moved to one of the cards at the bottom of another column. But all the cards below that card will come with it; so you will often have to move more than one card at a time—sometimes as many as a whole column of unrelated faceup cards.

Turn up the facedown cards as they become cleared and add them to the cards available to play. Try to expose the facedown cards as quickly as possible. When there are no more facedown cards in a pile, and you move the faceup card, you can fill that space only with an available King.

Scoring for Yukon is traditionally done in rounds of five games. Add up the number of foundation cards you've come up with in each round for your final score.

This game, with exactly the same layout, is known as Russian Solitaire, when the sequences built aat the bottom of the columns are descending *following suit;* otherwise played exactly the same way, Russian Solitaire is considered by some people to be the most difficult solitaire game.

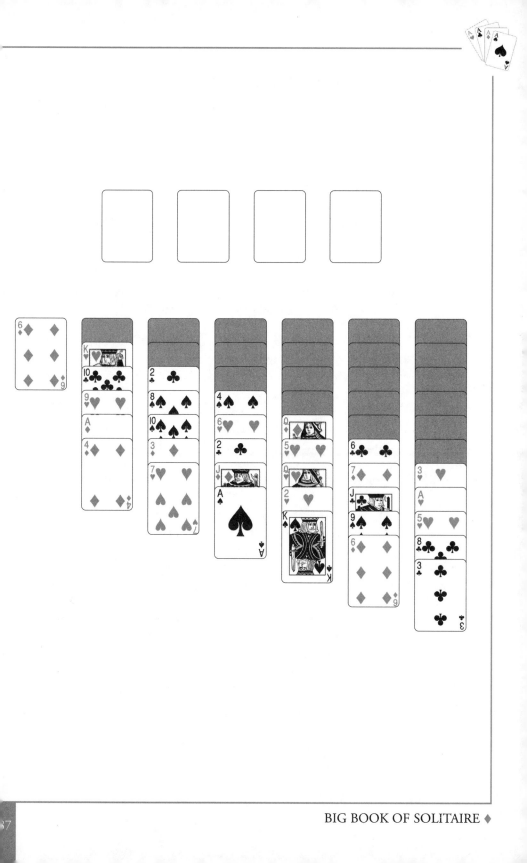

BIBLIOGRAPHICAL CURIOSITIES

In 1870, the first book on solitaire was printed as the *Illustrated Games of Patience* by Lady Adelaide Cadogan. Her work was reprinted so many times that solitaire games were even referred to as Cadogan or Patience. Her example was followed by Mrs. E. D. Cheney, an American, who the following year published *Patience,* and by Annie B. Henshaw, who published *Amusements for Invalids.*

The publishing house Dick & Fitzgerald of New York then published a first series of books dedicated to solitaires and patience games in 1883: The series was edited as *Dick's Games of Patience,* a second series being published by the same publisher in 1898.

Toward the end of the 19th century, such books on solitaire became popular, and articles on solitaires appeared in a multitude of popular publications, from *Popular Illustrations* to the first editions of the *Sunday Courier.*

The title of Annie B. Henshaw's work, as cited above, helps us understand that, at the beginning of this interest, solitaire was considered a game for invalids. Its function as a pastime for the less fortunate excused the game from any accusations of sinfulness that card playing had engendered from it earliest days. In Puritan American Society there was the need for such an alibi to let the "sinful" cards into households.

Accounts of card games also began to appear in the writings of well-known novelists. Already by 1880, to give just one example, Tolstoy (1828–1910) had included a solitaire game in a passage in his novel *War and Peace.* Also, Dostoyevsky (1821–1881), in *The Brothers Karamazov,* had his character Grushenka play solitaire in order to overcome moments of tension and uncertainty or for "passing time pleasantly and having fun."

Maybe this is the true reason why solitaire has been so successful: it is a pastime, but also a way in which to occupy one's mind, escaping worries, as one becomes fully absorbed in trying to make the game succeed.

INDEX